10 MINUTE
Acoustic Guitar
Workout

This edition © 2010 Omnibus Press
(A Division of Music Sales Ltd)
14-15 Berners Street, London W1T 3LJ, UK

Exclusive Distributors:
Music Sales Limited
Distribution Centre, Newmarket Road,
Bury St Edmunds, Suffolk IP33 3YB, UK
Music Sales Corporation
257 Park Avenue South, New York, NY10010
United States Of America
Macmillan Distribution Services
56 Parkwest Drive,
Derrimut Vic 3000, Australia

Order No. OP53141
ISBN 978-1-84938-076-8

© Copyright 2006, David Mead
published under exclusive licence by Omnibus Press, part of The Music Sales Group.
The Author hereby asserts his/her right to be identified as the author of this work in
accordance with Sections 77 to 78 of the Copyright, Designs and Patents Act 1988.

Page make-up by eMC Design
www.emcdesign.org.uk

All photographs courtesy of Carol Farnworth except image of Gordon Giltrap
(courtesy of Steve Catlin/Redferns).

www.musicsales.com

10 MINUTE
Acoustic Guitar
Workout

David Mead

BOOK CONTENTS

CD CONTENTS

CD recorded and produced by Martin Holmes at RDDM Ltd, Box, Wiltshire.

David Mead used a Yamaha LLX 500C acoustic guitar with Elixir strings.

Outro music 'Time Together' from David Mead's album 'Nocturnal' - check www.davidmead.net for details.

ACKNOWLEDGEMENTS

My thanks to everyone at Music Sales, especially Chris Harvey and Bob Wise. Thanks also to Martin Holmes for a great-sounding CD and totally painless recording experience, to Yamaha for the very fine LLX 500C acoustic guitar I used on the accompanying CD and to Alastair Pitcairn at Elixir for the excellent strings.

Thanks also to my sons, Tim and Toby, and to Carol, who is behind me every step of the way.

FOREWORD

by Gordon Giltrap

As a young amateur guitar player, the first album I ever bought was *With The Beatles* and the second was the first release by the legendary Bert Jansch, way back in 1965. It wasn't just the material on that first Jansch album that was life-changing for me; it was the *sound* of his haunting acoustic-guitar work that would play a very important part in my growth as a fledgling guitarist. Sure, I'd heard the sound of acoustic guitars in the hands of people like Dylan, Donovan and Peter, Paul And Mary, but it was the sound that Bert Jansch created that left a lifelong indelible mark on me. From that moment on, the acoustic guitar became my first and last love (apart from my human loved ones, of course!) in whatever form it takes, be it the six- or 12-string variety.

The main fascination it's held for me has always been the idea of it being a portable orchestra, a complete range of instruments in itself. Certainly, great players like Bert Jansch, Davy Graham and John Renbourn proved that point 40-plus years ago.

For me, the acoustic guitar has its own inbuilt healing properties, and when I try to explain to people that playing acoustic guitar is good for one's mental health, they look at me as if I'm mad! For that, I can't really blame them, but I know in my heart that this instrument has single-handedly kept me sane over the years, and each time I pick it up and get lost for hours in its inner sonic qualities, I'm reminded why I decided to make a career out of playing the acoustic guitar all those years ago.

So go into a quiet room, tune up and take yourself to another place, assisted by the knowledge contained in this superb book. I congratulate you, Mr Mead!

Gordon Giltrap
Summer 2006

INTRODUCTION

Way back in 1998 I wrote a book called *10 Minute Guitar Workout*. Well, it was originally called *Guitar Workout For The Interminably Busy*, but that title lasted only for the first edition, book publishers being notoriously squeamish about five-syllable words on their covers.

The original *10 Minute Guitar Workout* was aimed at guitarists who had busy lives and virtually no time left for practice, a syndrome I encountered often during my long years as a private guitar tutor – so often, in fact, that I became quite adept at giving my busier students a kind of condensed practice routine to ensure that their technical edge remained sharp and that they continued to progress. Acquiring a good technique is a great enabler when you're learning a musical instrument, as it allows you much speedier access to the material you're learning. After all, if you can pick up songs and pieces fairly quickly because your technique is good, there's less chance that you'll get bored, frustrated and tempted to give up.

To my surprise, *10 Minute Guitar Workout* caught on and became something of a bestseller, and people emailed me from all over the world to let me know how they were progressing with the exercises it contained. I followed it up with *Basic Guitar Workout*, which contained even more exercises and was intended to be a sort of 'I Ching' exercise routine where one task was taken at random by the student from each of the book's three sections every day and employed as part of a warm-up or wake-up call at the start of a practice routine.

It's taken me a while to come around to writing such a book intended solely for acoustic players. It occurred to me that, whereas the disciplines and rigours of playing the acoustic are similar to those of playing the electric guitar, there are major differences in the fine-tuning of technique – hence the *10 Minute Acoustic Guitar Workout*'s presence on the bookshelves.

Recent years have seen a kind of renaissance in acoustic playing, with many informed critics heralding this particular area of guitar music as being currently the most innovative. Technology has played its role, too, with acoustic guitars becoming increasingly concert-friendly thanks to the benefits of onboard electronics compliant with public address systems. Gone are the days when an acoustic guitarist was rooted to the spot in front of a microphone for fear of being rendered inaudible should he or she dare to move!

This is all good, as I personally love acoustic-guitar music and believe it to be an extremely fertile area of guitar playing where there is still new ground to cover, boundaries to be crossed and discoveries to be made. I hope that this book helps you to explore this marvellous terrain for yourself and aids you in becoming the musician you want to be.

David Mead
Summer 2006

HOW TO USE THIS BOOK

This book is divided into three parts. Part 1 is intended to be a general reference section and covers many of the topics associated with learning – everything from choosing strings to arranging songs. The chapters in this part are set out so that they can be read sequentially or dipped into individually. It's up to you.

The second part of the book contains a series of graduated exercises designed to improve and enhance your stamina and technique. The idea of a ten-minute-per-day exercise routine isn't exactly my own; it's based on a handbook issued years ago by the Canadian Air Force. This particular book guaranteed a level of physical fitness for the modern businessperson with no time or inclination to visit the gym. I tried it and it worked, and so, several years later, I thought that the same basic idea could easily be applied to learning the guitar. In this section, you'll be practising against the clock, which adds the edge of competition to what might be otherwise a fairly dull procedure.

For a long time, it's been my opinion – based on over 25 years' teaching experience – that people don't practise; they *noodle*. In other words, the average practice session tends to be entirely directionless and progress becomes stifled. You need to adopt a disciplined yet fun daily practice routine like the one descirbed in this book if you want to turn things around and begin progressing. The exercises in Part 2 have a lot of bite and you should start to see results fairly quickly.

The book ends with a very brief Part 3 that explores one of the guitar adventurer's most often-asked questions, 'How good is good enough?', and examines the question of how much work you need to put into learning a song or a piece before it's good enough to unleash on the public.

Lastly, I believe in offering all of my students a sort of 'after-sales service', so if there are any questions on the exercises you need answering or any points raised in this book that remain unclear to you, feel free to visit my website at www.davidmead.net and drop me a line. I'll do my best to help!

PART 1

EVERYTHING YOU NEED TO
KNOW ABOUT...

NOTATION

Reading Tab

It would be my guess that you're probably already familiar with the various ways in which guitar music is written down these days, but I thought it might be a good idea to cover the basics, just in case you're in need of a quick refresher. In any case, here's a guide to the notation used in this book.

The diagrams are split into about four different formats, as follows:

- Standard notation
- Tablature
- Chord boxes
- Fretboard diagrams.

Let's consider each of these in turn.

Standard Notation

Don't worry; you don't need to be able to read music to be able to work through the chapters and charts in this book. Really, I'm including standard notation only because I think it's important to have a reference to what music looks like out there in the real world. In fact, I've always believed that you need to learn to read music only if it's going to be useful to you. If, for instance, you want to try your hand at playing in professional music circles, with the aim of honing your skills to become a session player or accompanist, then yes, perhaps you should learn how to read standard notation. There's no getting away from the fact that it's the official language of the professional music world and, like the language of any place in which you intend to spend some time, it's a good idea to have at least enough vocabulary to cover the basics. Being able to read a simple melody line in standard notation can be a lifesaver, as it can help you fill in those inevitable memory blanks that occur when you're learning a new song. Plus, of course, you won't find tablature for everything you want to play.

Naturally, I'm not going to teach you to read music in just a few paragraphs – after all, it's not really what we're here for – but just to whet your appetite, here are a few pointers.

First of all, the music stave we use for guitar notation looks like this:

The squiggly symbol on the left-hand side is known as the *treble clef* or *G clef* (named after the note on the stave around which the squiggle in the middle is drawn) and is there to let everyone know the order of notes on display. In fact, there are numerous clefs in music – more than you could shake a stick at, in fact – but luckily we need concern ourselves only with this one. Not every instrument is so lucky, however; pianists have to be able to read two different clefs – traditionally, one for each hand – and so as guitar players we're really quite fortunate in this respect.

You might have been taught in school that the notes on the lines of the stave (the range of five horizontal stacked lines following on from the clef) spell out E G B D F, bottom to top, and the notes in the spaces spell FACE. Well, that's one way to look at things, but I think it's more logical to take the approach that the bottom line is E and then we proceed up the musical scale alphabetically until we reach the top, like this:

E   F   G   A   B   C   D   E   F

Here are those notes in place:

Thinking this way means that you don't have to remember mnemonics (memory aids) like the phrase 'Every Good Boy Deserves Football' in order to learn the notes on the lines.

If we run out of lines and spaces, we merely make some more. However, in order to keep things tidy, we don't draw them right across the page; instead, we add them to each individual note, like this:

This particular note is an A, and you'll find that it fits into the music alphabet perfectly if we continue from where we left off:

The same goes for notes lower than the bottom line, too:

This particular note is the lowest we can play on a guitar tuned to standard tuning (ie E A D G B E, low to high) and is produced when the bottom string is plucked when it's open (ie unfretted).

As I've already said, we're going to cover only the basics of reading here. If you're set on bringing your reading skills up to scratch, there are plenty of books on the market that will help you out.

Other symbols you're likely to find on the music staff (another name for the stave) within these pages include this one:

It looks like a fraction, doesn't it? In fact, it's known as a *time signature* and it tells the music reader that there are four beats in this particular section of music – known as a *bar* – and that each of these beats is a quarter note in length.

If the top number changes, it tells us a different story:

Here, the time signature indicates that the bar contains three beats, each of which is a quarter note in length.

This kind of information concerns rhythm, something I'm not going to spend a lot of time talking about here. If you're curious, check out another book of mine, the one titled *Rhythm*, which will tell you everything you need to know about the topic.

Here's another important pair of symbols:

The one by the note on the left, looking like a kind of baroque lower-case letter B, is known as a *flat* symbol, while its counterpart next to the note on the right is called a *sharp* symbol and looks like a hash mark. These two symbols are important in the language of music because the basic array of notes on the staff doesn't tell a full enough story. For instance, while you might know that the note on the third fret of your bass string is a G, as shown here in standard notation...

...what about the next note up the fretboard? Move your finger one fret to the right and you'll be playing G sharp (G♯), and so we have to be able to notate this without using another line or space. The solution is to write the note again in the same place but with a sharp symbol next to it, like this:

It's a similar story for the flat symbol. The note B flat (B♭) looks like this:

I realise that all of this might sound like advanced maths to you and nothing whatever to do with strumming Beatles songs, or whatever, but believe me, by spending just a few moments coming to terms with the rudiments of notation you'll be doing yourself a huge favour in the long run. As I said earlier, there are many books available that will come to your aid if you wish to pursue your music-reading studies, and so for brevity's sake we'll move on...

Tablature

Known to its friends as 'tab', tablature has been around for hundreds of years and was once the standard format for writing down music for a distant cousin of the guitar: the lute. There are manuscripts in tablature in the British Museum that date back to the time of Bach. It really is a very old system of notation!

The good thing about tab is that it's a dedicated system – ie, it applies only to the guitar. What's more, unlike standard notation, the basics of tab can be easily learned in just a few minutes.

Take a look at the photo of my guitar's neck below. The thick bass E string is at the bottom, so that the names of the open strings ascend up the picture – E A D G B E.

Tab represents the guitar neck with the bass string at the bottom

The basic tablature grid mimics this absolutely, offering a guitarist's-eye view of the fretboard:

Here, there are six lines, each representing one of the guitar's six strings. If I wanted you to play the same G note on the bass string we looked at earlier, all I'd have to do would be to tell you which fret number that note is located on, like this:

The figure 3 on the lowest line means that the note to be played is located on the lowest string at the third fret.

And that's really all there is to tab, believe it or not. We don't have to bother ourselves with ancillary symbols for sharps and flats, either. If I wanted you to play the G sharp

we looked at a moment ago, all I'd have to do is tell you which fret you'll find it on:

Simple, huh? If I wanted you to play a chord – or, at least, more than one note – all I'd need to do is pile the notes on top of each other:

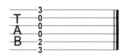

This is a simple G major chord, something with which I expect you're already quite familiar. It might take a while to work out where all the numbers are, but reading this kind of numbering is still a lot quicker than deciphering standard notation.

Later on in this book, you'll find standard notation and tab locked together to form a block, like this:

This is the way you're most likely to find guitar music printed in books and guitar magazines from all over the world, and so you should be starting to see that it makes a lot of sense to familiarise yourself and become comfortable with tab.

I do have one thing to add before we move on, though. Although tab might seem like the ultimate non-reading guitarists' resource for learning new songs and melodies, it has one fatal flaw: there is no facility in modern tablature for expressing rhythmic information. Way back in time when tab was first developed there was additional data squeezed onto the page, but over the years this has been phased out in favour of adopting a simpler approach. This means, of course, that it's difficult to learn a song or a piece of music from tab if you've never heard it before. While this isn't a problem with standard notation, as all the information required to play any piece – melodic, rhythmic and harmonic – is shown on the page, tab boasts only two out of these three fundamental criteria and so falls slightly short of being an all-inclusive system of notation.

Chord Boxes

As you've seen by now, it's an easy matter to notate chords in tablature, but most guitarists will agree that chords are far easier to grasp when they're depicted in a more pictorial manner – hence the chord box.

A basic chord box looks like this:

If you compare the diagram above to the picture at the top of the next column, you'll see a distinct similarity:

Chord boxes represent the guitar neck in this position, with the bass string on the left-hand side

Just as if you were looking directly at the guitar, in a chord box the bass strings are depicted on the left and the thinner treble strings on the right. If I wanted you to play a particular chord, I'd place spots on the strings corresponding to where you'd place your fingers, like this:

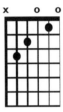

If you wanted to play the chord shown in the above diagram, you'd place the third finger of your left hand on the third fret, fifth string, your second finger on the second fret, fourth string, and finally your first finger on the first fret, second string.

You'll see that there are some letters above the diagram, too. An *x* above an open or unfretted string means that the string shouldn't be sounded in the chord, while an *o* indicates that you should strike or pluck the open string along with the other fretted notes. So, in the example above, you wouldn't sound the bass E string but you would include the third and top strings within the chord.

If the chord is to be played further up the guitar neck, instead of just elongating the diagram to incorporate more of the fretboard, a number is included to the left of the diagram to indicate the fret at which the chord is located:

Here, it's quite clear that the chord is to be played at the eighth fret.

Guitar players tend to learn chords and even scales by the shapes they make on the fretboard, and the way the instrument functions in a musical context certainly facilitates this. As you'll see shortly, nearly all scale and chord shapes are moveable – ie, each shape can be played at different locations on the fretboard – which means that you need to program the information into your memory only once. After that, it's a matter of working out the correct location for the scale or chord on the fretboard.

Fretboard Diagrams

These involve another system of notation, and they operate along very similar lines to chord boxes. In many ways, they're a cross between chord boxes and tablature.

Take a look at the picture below:

Fretboard diagrams offer a guitarist's-eye view of the fretboard

Once again, this is the guitar fretboard with the bass string at the bottom – similar to our perspective when we're holding the guitar in a playing position. Now, look at the following diagram:

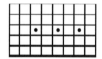

This sort of diagram is used to describe things like scale patterns. For instance, if I wanted to show you what kind of shape a C major scale makes at the eighth fret, I'd write this:

8 fret

This kind of diagram enables you to see the overall shape of the scale on the fretboard – and, as you'll see, this kind of visualisation is an important learning aid – but I would probably back it up with the same information in both tab and standard notation formats, like the diagram at the bottom of this page.

So now you have a representation of the same scale in three different forms of notation: standard notation, tab and fretboard diagram. If I wanted to get across some musical information that I thought was too tricky to convey using diagrams alone, I'd probably back it up with a photograph, too. This way, the margin for error is only very slight.

As I said at the beginning of this chapter, the chances are that this has been nothing more than a case of revision for most of you, as all the methods of notation we've looked at are fairly standard in printed guitar music. If we do come across anything else as we proceed towards the workout, I'll give you a full explanation at the appropriate moment.

C major scale in standard notation and tab

TUNING

During my years as a teacher, I've always made tuning my guitar the first job of the day. I made a point of tuning all my students' guitars for them at the start of a lesson, too, a task that served a dual purpose: not only did it mean that I could guarantee that we were going to start the lesson in tune with each other, but also that it was possible for me to assess how much practice the student had done by how in or out of tune his or her guitar was!

In this book, we're going to be concerning ourselves primarily with standard tuning – that is, the traditional method of classical guitar tuning, whereby the guitar is tuned like this:

E   A   D   G   B   E

Bass ◀────────────▶ **Treble**

This is also known in some circles as *Spanish tuning*, merely because it's the norm for classical, or Spanish, guitars.

You might have heard mention of special tunings for modern acoustic guitar music, whereby players tune their instrument to a chord or to some other mysterious alternative, such as D A D G A D. We'll be looking briefly at the sort of thing you can do with a few judicious turns of the tuning keys later on, but for now let's just think about getting the instrument in tune with itself.

If I was to make a list of rules for learning guitar, it's beyond doubt that number one would be this:

Never practise on an out-of-tune guitar!

Even in the early stages of learning, it's vital that everything you do actually has musical worth; chords should be perfectly in tune, scales should sound correct when played across the strings and melodies should be exactly as written and not slightly off. In all honesty, trying to do any valuable practice on an instrument that isn't spot-on in the tuning department is like trying to read with poorly adjusted glasses: it distorts the information you're trying to input

into your hands and fingers and certainly won't do your sense of pitch any good, either.

So the first job of any practice session is to tune your guitar – every time, no exceptions. Even if your initial strum tells you that there isn't a tuning issue present, check it anyway. While your ear is developing a good sense of pitch, it's quite probable that you'll mistake your instrument as being in tune even when it's actually ten per cent or more out of tune. The only way to sharpen your senses in this particular region is to keep checking until you're sure that everything is in order.

Of course, having said all this, I'd be the first to say that the guitar is a difficult instrument to keep in tune! Just about everything affects it. New strings, humidity, changes in room temperature, inadvertent knocks and bumps – all of these factors and many more can conspire to make playing a less than mellifluous experience.

So what's the best way to ensure that your instrument stays in tune? Well, if you'd asked me that question 20 years ago, I'd probably have said, 'By buying a tuning fork and learning to do things the hard way.' But I was a lot grumpier back then. Today, technology has progressed to the extent that there's a range of startlingly accurate acoustic-guitar tuners on the market. Most of them are battery-operated models fitted with a little built-in microphone that listens to each string and squirts a pulse of coded information into the onboard processor, which then tells you if the string is sharp or flat. Simple as that.

There's also a slightly more sophisticated breed of tuner on the market that clips onto the headstock of your guitar and checks its tuning from the internal vibrations that are produced when the instrument is played. In fact, I use one of these types of tuner, and while I have to admit that I haven't a clue as to how it works its tuning magic, I'd never be without it, either in the practice room or on the concert stage. But whichever type of tuner takes your fancy, my advice is simply to go out and buy one. You'll never believe your ears again!

ACOUSTIC GUITAR STRINGS

I get asked all the time about what type of string I think people should put on their acoustic guitars, and quite often my inquisitors aren't entirely happy with my answer.

The thing is that many people take up the acoustic guitar as a second instrument, their first being the electric guitar, and there's a whole raft of differences between the two in terms of approach, feel and general technique. If, for instance, you've spent a couple of years playing electric, you'll have become used to light-gauge strings and applying a fairly light touch when it comes to striking the strings, whereas playing the acoustic requires a rather heavier touch on heavier-gauge strings. It's a difference that I believe is similar to that between playing electronic keyboards and acoustic piano – the 'touch' is altogether different, and swapping between the two calls for some considerable re-orienteering. So, when it comes down to talking about strings – the most fundamental piece of kit you can buy for any guitar – most electric players are quite shocked when they experience how the transition from thin strings to the heartier-gauge ones used by acoustic players can affect their performance.

The differences don't end with thicker strings, either; acoustic guitars quite often have higher playing actions, too. (The term *action* in this context refers to the height of the strings above the fretboard.) I'll show you what I mean. Here's a picture of an electric guitar's action:

Electric guitars often have slimmer necks and lower actions than acoustics

You can see that there's not much of a gap between the wood of the fretboard and the strings above it. Now look at an acoustic guitar's action:

Acoustic guitars generally have higher playing actions than solid-body electric guitars

It's not radically higher – certainly not as high as some of the actions on guitars of yore. I don't want to come on like some wise old guy with a long grey beard, sitting in the corner of a bar and starting every sentence with the words 'When I was young...' and looking continuously wistful, but when I *was* young some makes of acoustic guitar were worthy of being adopted by the Spanish Inquisition as instruments of torture. I suffered at the hands of such an instrument, as did many of my contemporaries, and nearly lost all my left-hand fingerprints as a result. Blisters? Sometimes I woke up screaming.

Seriously though, folks, I've heard many players say that, despite the pain and strain that the acoustics of the '70s put us through, it was worth it for the extra finger strength that all the additional exertion produced.

I disagree. I belong to the school of thought that rules out the assumed benefits of poorly wrought instruments or poor set-ups on acoustic guitars and would go on to say that, if the height of the strings at the 12th fret of your instrument measures in at 1cm (approx $^7/_{16}$ of an inch) or more, you should seek professional assistance from a qualified guitar tech. Don't grin and bear it. Get it fixed.

So electric players who migrate towards the charms of the acoustic sometimes find that higher playing actions and thicker strings get in the way a little. The solution?

There isn't one, I'm afraid. Both of these characteristics of acoustic-guitar life are there for a reason and are essential to the way that the instrument sounds. I'll try to explain without becoming unnecessarily entangled with science...

We all know that if you tighten a piece of string between two points and pluck it, the result is a pitch that's relative to the tension present in the string and its length. (This is only meant to be a thumbnail sketch, remember; I'm a musician, not a physicist.) It doesn't matter if the 'string' is made from metal or nylon; the trick regarding the ratio of pitch and length still works. Obviously, the various materials used in the manufacture of different types of string will affect the *timbre** of the note.

Another thing that will have an effect on the pitch and quality of the note a string produces is the thickness of the string itself. Very basically, the thicker the string, the better and louder the resulting pitch. Different thicknesses are found to be best for various ranges of notes in the musical spectrum, and it's for this fundamental reason that strings come in numerous gauges. The high E on your guitar might be as thin as .008" and might increase to .013" or .014", for instance. And while these might appear like statistics that are measurable only with a micrometer, the ear – and certainly the fingers – can readily detect them, too.

Needless to say, a gauge of .008" is considered to be useful or practical only as a string for an electric guitar, whose pick-ups electromagnetically detect the vibrations before feeding them to an amplifier, where they are, unsurprisingly, amplified before being reproduced through a speaker. In other words, the electric side of the instrument actually helps out here and means that an electric-guitar player can get away with using far lighter gauges of string than his or her acoustic-playing counterpart.

If you were to try a .008" string on an acoustic guitar, the note it produced would sound thin and its tone would be very poor. This is because the way an acoustic guitar makes a note has a lot to do with the stimulation of air within the body of the instrument and the sympathetic vibration of the different woods that feature in its construction. Quite simply, producing a good tone on an acoustic requires more of a 'push' from a thicker string. This is why acoustic-guitar string sets usually start with a top E string measuring in at .010" – and these are referred to as being 'ultra-light gauge'! In my opinion, you shouldn't really consider anything thinner than a .011" string for a top E, promising yourself that one day you'll at least try a far more manly .012". It might take a while to get used to, and you might have to resign yourself to another batch of sore fingers, but the improvement in the general tone and timbre of the notes you produce will be

worth all the slight inconveniences. It's my bet that you'll want to increase the string gauge on your electric afterwards, too!

So, now that I've hopefully explained one of the major differences in 'feel factor' between an electric and acoustic guitar, let's look briefly at the other: string height. The difference between the actions of acoustic and electric guitars is fairly simple to explain; with the strings on the latter being thicker and requiring the player to play them with greater force in order to produce a good dynamic range, they need more space to vibrate than the strings of an electric. If you have an electric guitar, try playing a few chords on it and then swap over and play the same thing on an acoustic. You should find that your touch on the electric tends to be lighter than on the acoustic, where your right hand needs to play harder.

The extra string height of an acoustic guitar will obviously mean you'll have to press harder with the fingers of your left hand, especially when playing above the fifth or seventh frets. But while this might feel like quite a considerable impediment to begin with, it isn't such a hard thing to become used to. And you can console yourself with the knowledge that all the hard work involved in orientating yourself in your new playing environment will be worth it in the end.

String Types

Obviously, there's a host of different makes of string on the market, and I'm not going to begin choosing a brand for you. Every player will tell you that his or her choice of string manufacturer has been made after years of trying out everything available and settling on one make in particular – and then sticking with it out of a thing known in the trade as *brand loyalty*. If I was to offer advice on choosing a brand, I'd say that it's a safe bet to go for a major manufacturer, and a quick flick through any guitar magazine will reveal who these are. You might also find yourself steered towards a particular brand by reading interviews with established players, which is all well and good; if you've heard a recording of someone whose tone you admire, it's always good to do a little research and find out what kind of hardware and accessories he or she is using. (Be aware, though, that their choice of hardware is probably less than half the story, as far as good tone is concerned. As we'll see later on in the book, the main factor behind a nice guitar sound is a good playing technique.)

Other choices you'll have to make while you stand there in the guitar shop, perusing the string section, is whether or not to go for a coated string. The coating of strings is a fairly recent innovation in string technology and involves applying a micro-thin layer of some kind of protective agent

* Timbre is just a fancy music word that means 'quality of tone'.

to the wound strings (ie the low E, A, D and G strings) that impedes their natural deterioration. The prime cause of string wear is corrosion from sweaty fingers (disgusting, I know, but true), and the protective agent can slow this down significantly without affecting the string's tone.

The apparent downside of coating strings is that strings treated in this way tend to be more expensive than the non-coated variety, but many players attest that the resulting extra life and longer-lasting tone make the extra cost worth paying in the end. Coated strings tend to be quieter, too, inasmuch as you tend to produce less of a 'squeal' as you change positions on the fretboard than with their non-coated counterparts. (I have to add at this point that I'm a great fan of coated strings and use them all the time!)

As for the other variations between the different makes of string that are currently available, you'll find that these are down mainly to the type of material or creative process employed by their individual manufacturers. You'll see names like 'Phosphor', 'Phosphor Bronze', 'Silk Wrapped Core' and so on. The way in which all music strings work, however, is fundamentally the same, and all the differences between the various types of string tend to be merely variations on a theme. In the initial experimental stages, as you try out different types of string, you'll probably find that you get through many different strings by different manufacturers before you find a brand that suits your playing style or just feels right. Once again, there's no harm in being influenced by hearsay or things you read in interviews with established players; we all rely on the 'jungle line' to a certain extent to help us form our own conclusions.

String Life

Another question that tends to crop up a lot in the seminars I hold is 'How do I know when it's time to change my guitar strings?' Let's deal with this one here and now.

When you put a fresh set of strings on a guitar, they're perfectly round (or as near as dammit, at least) and spotlessly clean, too. So you have two pieces of (almost) cylindrical wire – the unwound top E and B strings – and four strings that are wrapped with extra wire to give them the extra girth needed to produce the range of tones called for at their various tensions. After you've tuned your guitar, the virgin metal will stretch and settle for a while, and it will take some time before they begin to remain stable at pitch. As you play, those perfect cylinders start to bash around on the metal frets, which obviously has an effect on their shape and subsequently their ability to perform well at pitch. Other factors affect the string, too: the constant vibration they sustain causes the inevitable onset of metal fatigue, and as I said earlier the corrosive influence of sweat from your fingertips will begin to tarnish and discolour them.

In a perfect world, of course, all these events could be factored together to produce an equation that would enable us to calculate the life expectancy of a string, but there are simply too many variables involved for us to be able to do so.

To begin with, it must be fairly obvious that a string is going to die more quickly if you play your guitar all the time. Not so obvious, though, is the fact that your actual style of playing can be a factor as well. No two players will strike the string with exactly the same velocity (which in this case equates to force) or add vibrato at the same level or even sweat to the same degree when they play. All this means is that it's almost impossible to say things like, 'Oh, a set of new strings should last you three months.' As a general guide, though, the things to watch out for are:

- **Discolouration** – When the silver colour of the top strings and the brass or bronze colour of the lower strings starts to look patchy, there's a good chance that you'll need to start planning a visit to the guitar store for fresh strings.

- **Tuning Inconsistency** – As I said earlier, the constant bashing of metal strings against the metal frets causes the strings to lose their cylindrical shape, which affects their ability to vibrate symmetrically, which in turn can lead to all sorts of tuning aberrations. If you've had your strings for a while and you find your guitar difficult to tune, it's probably time for a change.

- **Loss Of Timbre** – As a string grows old and tired, the factors listed above conspire together to the extent that it begins to lose tone, which shows up as a loss of treble or, at least, brightness. This can be very difficult to spot, however, because the decrease in tone is very gradual and will probably remain unnoticed (I've played students' guitars whose strings sound like old rubber bands rather than singing metal), so watch out for this. Take a good listen to your strings: if they're beginning to sound like they've got a bad head cold, change them.

- **Corrosion** – People don't believe me when I tell them that I've had students come to me with guitars that had *rusty* strings on them – not just discoloured but black and rusty, and often with great stalactites of dirt hanging from them, too. I needn't tell you that a clean string is a healthy string, and for this reason it's a good habit to wipe them occasionally, the same as you'd (hopefully) clean any other work surface. Naturally, when things get to the state where you can actually feel the corrosion on the surface of the string, you're way past the time for a string change.

- **Breakage** – There is a school of thought that reasons that poor playing technique is more likely to cause string breakage than anything else. Well, it's certain that wild, frenzied bashing-about will cause death by breakage quicker than anything, but I wouldn't go as far as to say that this particular law is absolute. It's true that, if you're continually breaking strings, something is definitely wrong with either your technique or your guitar, but everyone is prone to the occasional mishap where musical metal is concerned. However, if you break a string and it's been a while since the last string change, it might be a good idea to change all of the strings, not just the single casualty. Otherwise, you might find yourself open to all sorts of tonal inconsistencies due to mismatched strings.

Guidelines For A Successful String Change

To begin with, buy yourself a string winder, like this one:

A string winder: one of the most useful inventions ever!

Not only will such a device save you from suffering with sore wrists through continually turning your tuning pegs, but most string winders also come with an invaluable tool. The little notch pictured below is for taking out the string pegs on the guitar's bridge and will save you much frustration and cursing while looking around the house to find a suitable alternative.

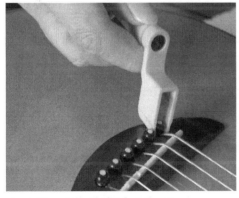

The notch at the upper edge of the string winder fits over the string peg to aid removal during a string change

It's best to change the strings one at a time (unless you have any other spring-cleaning duties to perform, like mucking out the fretboard), starting with the bass E. There's no reason why you should start here, really, but I always do and so it sounds right to me.

Be careful when you extract the string pegs; they're made of quite sturdy plastic but do tend to break if subjected to rough handling. If you're nervous about breaking one, hoof it down to the local guitar store and buy a couple of spares to keep in your guitar case as insurance. They cost only a few pence each and you really shouldn't be without them. You'll also find pegs manufactured from other materials – wood, brass, synthetic ivory and so on – each claiming to enhance the tone of your guitar. I haven't had any experience of this, as I've stuck with plastic ones, but feel free to experiment with other types as the alternatives are all very modestly priced.

Despite all the advances in luthiery – the art of guitar manufacture and maintenance – over the years, string pegs are still very low-tech. Essentially, all they do is act as wedges or bungs to keep the strings in place at the bridge, so it will be a little while before you get used to handling them. To use one in a string-changing situation, thread the string through the hole in the guitar bridge, insert the peg and give it a few gentle tugs to make sure it's holding fast. It's not unusual for the string to slip a little here as you tighten it to pitch, and in fact I've even had string pegs take off like missiles during a hasty string change and have ended up looking under furniture and doing fingertip searches on dark carpets to find them. The old adage 'more haste, less speed' should be considered here; take things slowly and give the seated peg the occasional press while you take the string up to pitch and all should be well.

When it comes to removing old strings from guitars, I find it's a good habit to coil the old one up and put it in the packet you've taken the new string from immediately, as not only does this keep it safe (and you'd be surprised how difficult it is to find a carelessly discarded string on a carpet) but it also keeps everything neat and tidy.

Tying the string around the capstan at the headstock is a tricky business and takes the average guitarist a few string-changes to master the technique. What you have is a brand new string – clean, shiny and, therefore, slippery – that you have to anchor somehow around a metal shaft with a hole in it. Again, experience is your best friend here, and I recommend that you watch someone change the strings for you for the first time and literally show you the ropes. Failing that, when you get around to fixing your replacement string, try to follow these guidelines:

- Your new strings will nearly always be too long for your

guitar. This is because some guitars – Epiphones, for instance – have very long headstocks, and string manufacturers obviously want to follow the 'one size fits all' rule as far as possible, so you're going to need a pair of good quality wire cutters to trim your strings to length. Pliers will do the trick, too, but using them is a little clumsy in this situation so it's best to equip yourself with the right tool for the job and pay a visit to your local hardware store. In some locations, wire cutters are known as 'piano wire cutters' (although I've never known anyone brave enough to cut piano wire with them!), and you'll also find other types dedicated to cutting the soft copper wire used for electrical work, although these really aren't up to the job of cutting guitar strings.

- Gauging exactly how much guitar string you need to wrap around the capstan is a skilled job, but you don't need any more than about three turns to anchor the string well. Any more than that and the string begins to wrap over itself on the capstan, which can cause tuning instability, so take the time to make sure you get this right. Here's a helpful picture showing what a well-planted string looks like at the headstock end:

Untidy windings lead to tuning instability, so try to aim for two or three neat turns of the string around the capstan, as shown here

- Don't cut the string to length before inserting it through the capstan; instead, leave the trimming process to the end and do all of the strings at once. It's very inadvisable to leave string ends flapping around the headstock untrimmed because they can actually do a lot of damage. I know a few guitarists who have inadvertently hit themselves in the eye with a runaway string.

- Thread the string through the hole and make a bend in it on the other side and then turn the tuning key slowly, trying to keep a finger on the string to guide it up the post. It's a good idea here to lock the string

into position with some tight turns. Don't allow it to slacken off, as this will result in what's known as a *loose wrap*, which might cause you problems when tuning up.

It's probably true to say that just about everyone makes a bit of a hash of their first string change, so don't worry if you end up with something that looks like day one at Boy Scout camp; learn from your mistakes and you'll soon be doing Formula One-grade string changes every time.

Once the new string is in place and tuned to pitch, run your finger underneath it and pull it out from the fretboard a little to stretch it, like this:

Stretching a new string by running your finger along its length once or twice helps it stretch and settle in

Doing this will save you some laborious extra tuning, as new strings all start to stretch like crazy from the point that they're tensioned up. You don't need to do anything too physical; simply running your finger under the whole playing length of the string a couple of times is generally all that's called for.

You'll find that the guitar probably needs tuning two or three times before its pitch begins to stabilise. I generally let an instrument rest for a few hours after I've changed the strings in order to give the new set a chance to bed in. Strictly speaking, this isn't absolutely necessary; it's just a habit I've got into. Nonetheless, I find that, if a newly strung guitar is given a bit of time off, it tends to hold its tuning much better than it otherwise would.

EAR TRAINING

There are many guitar players out there who spend an awful lot of time and money looking after their instruments and yet don't spend any time at all on their most valuable, home-grown asset: their ears.

Realistically, ear training is all about becoming familiar with the basic currency of music – that is to say that music comprises 12 notes, repeated over and over again, beginning at a very low pitch and ending very high. Loosely speaking, the actual range of music, low to high, is governed by the way that we *hear* music; we can't hear below a certain pitch – as bass notes get lower and lower, there's a point beyond which we detect them as nothing more than a vibration or a rumble. In fact, home cinema sound systems operate on this principle: the bass speakers handle the low notes but it's left to the subwoofer to belt out the super-low frequencies that represent cruising spaceships, explosions, thunderstorms and so on. These particular sounds can still be defined musically as having frequencies and, hence, pitches; it's just that we don't hear them that way.

It's the same story at the other end of the music spectrum, too; there's a certain pitch above which we can't hear. This critical frequency varies from person to person – older people, for instance, are less able to hear higher frequencies then someone in their 20s – but just because we can't hear a sound doesn't mean that it's not actually there, of course. Just ask any well-spoken bat, dog or cat about high frequencies and you'll hear a completely different story.

In general, our range of hearing covers the frequencies from 20Hz (that's Hertz, pronounced 'hurts', the unit of measurement for frequency) to 20,000Hz, but that's in scientific terms and not really of much use to us here. In real terms, this range spans around ten and a bit octaves, but the top-end frequencies are well above the top notes on most instruments you could name me. For instance, the range of the average symphony orchestra tends to be from around 40Hz to 14,000Hz – a range of approximately eight

and a half octaves. A piano, meanwhile, covers between seven and eight octaves, depending on the make and model, while the average acoustic guitar covers just over three octaves. All very interesting stuff, I'm sure you'll agree, but I don't want to turn this into a scientific treatise on the human ability to discern frequency; I'm just trying to put things into perspective for you.

So, if the guitar has to deal with only three and a bit octaves, the chromatic scale repeats itself only three and a bit times on the instrument, from the lowest note on the bass E (82Hz) to the uppermost C on the top string (1,047 Hz). This is the musical range over which we have to train our ears to specialise, of course, although a general overview of the musical spectrum helps here, too.

I think it's fair to say that virtually every musician begins his or her musical life in need of some ear training. That's not to say that we all begin with absolute tone-deafness, of course, but most of us tend to start with horrendously inaccurate blunderbusses on either side of our heads and face the job of refining things to the level of sniper-sharp marksmen over time. Obviously this takes work – conscious work – and it's never enough just to let things lie in the hope that our sense of hearing will advance hand in hand with our general musical understanding.

Ear training is really all about musical awareness, and knocking yours into shape in this regard will have a direct effect on your ability to speak and understand the language of music. Without it, your powers as a musician will remain under-developed and incomplete, without the sharpness of focus required for performing at a professional level.

So, if understanding music from an aural point of view means coming to terms with the actual currency of music, we need to be able to appreciate its various denominations, by which I'm referring to *intervals*, from the smallest to the highest. It's like knowing how to handle any currency: how many cents in a dime? How many in a euro? Knowing the answers to both questions would obviously make transactions conducted in both currencies far easier to understand, and the same can be said for music. In Western music, the smallest denomination is called a *semitone* – that's the musical distance from one fret on your guitar to the next – and the largest is an octave, which is a 12-fret distance. Along the way, there are various other units that are all made up from groups of semitones and have different sounds and functions as part of the general run of music. You might have come across terms like 'major third' or 'perfect fifth', for instance. These merely express distances along the scale, and you'll be learning more about them later on, so don't worry too much for now about the unusual and somewhat cumbersome terms involved in music's language just yet; I'll try to cover everything that'll be useful to you by the end of the book.

In my experience, there are two types of ear training that have to be addressed. One is the general one undertaken by all musicians and involves the task of learning how to identify intervals, scale relationships, arpeggios, chord types and so on. The other is a far more localised form and involves gaining the ability to rationalise all this data and process it, and for guitarists this needs to be done in direct relation to their instruments. Different instruments have vastly different musical characteristics, of course, as well as diverse musical ranges and idiosyncrasies galore, so gaining the ability to recognise basic musical information as it concerns your own instrument is vital.

Many players take a blasé approach to ear training, deciding that it either isn't that important or that they'll just pick it up as they go along, but this simply isn't the case. You'll be able to make a great deal of progress on the instrument if you put aside some time to work on your ears – and training them up can be fun, too.

Many years ago, when I was teaching one-on-one lessons, I used to play pitch-recognition games with my students in order to train up their sense of the relationships between notes. Today, there are computer programs available that do essentially the same job, and a simple internet search should pinpoint many examples of these. Fundamentally, they all the work in the same way: by providing an interface that allows the user to determine his or her own parameters of learning. For instance, if you want to concentrate on learning the intervals of a major scale, you can instruct the program to limit itself to a single octave and play only those intervals. Then, as your ear develops, you can increase the program's scope accordingly.

The good news is that most of these programs are available as shareware, and so cost very little, and they're often operational for trial periods, during which you can explore cut-down or 'lite' versions of the full program,

giving you the opportunity to find the one that best suits your temperament.

I'd advise you to spend some time in tracking down such a program and then scheduling some time each day to play with it. As with everything, if you take measured steps with a graduated level of difficulty, you'll see progress being made after only a short time.

Here's the best way to proceed. To begin with, you need to be able to recognise the difference between major and minor chords and scales. This difference is fundamental to the whole span of music; every chord, scale or arpeggio is basically either major or minor at its core, and if you can develop the ability to discern between the two then this will serve as a solid foundation upon which to build your musical awareness.

Set the program so that it plays you a series of chords or arpeggios in both major and minor forms and test your ability to differentiate between them. At the same time, spend some time with the intervals of the major scale and learn to tell them apart by having the computer play the root note and a random interval above it. Begin with the simple intervals – scale tones, no chromatic notes – and learn to hear their unique characteristics. Here are some guidelines.

You should be able to accelerate your learning of the intervals of a major scale by personalising the process a little. If, for instance, you're struggling to remember the sound made by a root note and the fourth above it – for instance the notes C and F in the C major scale...

```
C   D   E   F
1   2   3   4
```

...try to think of a melody that begins with these two notes. Two that spring to my mind are 'The British Grenadiers', which is a military band march, and the first two notes of the theme tune to the UK TV series *Blackadder*. If I'm ever unsure what a fourth sounds like, all I have to do is recall either of these two tunes and hey presto! Problem solved. Over the years, various students of mine have come up with many tunes in order to help them remember the intervals of the major scale. Here's a small selection:

- **Major second** – 'Frère Jacques'
- **Major third** – 'The Blue Danube' waltz by Johann Strauss II
- **Perfect fifth** – The theme to *Star Wars*
- **Major sixth** – 'My Bonnie Lies Over The Ocean'
- **Major seventh** – This is a tricky one because virtually no melody starts with these two notes as they are recognised as very difficult for a singer to pitch, one

after the other. Personally, I remember this interval because it's contained in the first four notes of the jazz standard 'I Can't Get Started'. If you know of any others, please email me!

After sorting out the intervals of the major scale, you should move on and start working on being able to differentiate between the various different types of scale – and there are many to choose from. You can get as exotic as you like here, and you'll never be short of examples to choose from. Basically, recognising scales is a matter of hearing the order in which the basic intervals of music are presented.

Nearly all scales are made up from tones and semitones (that's the distance between two frets and one fret, respectively, on your guitar fretboard) in various combinations, and so the ability to hear these basic intervals is essential. I go into more detail on scale construction in the 'Scales' chapter but for now here's a brief rundown of the basics along with a few exercises, giving you the chance to play something on your guitar and actually hear what I mean.

To begin with, the reason why major and minor scales or chords sound different lies with the third note of the scale, which is different in each. In a major chord, the relationship between the root and the third sounds like this:

In a minor chord, the interval separating the root and the third is one semitone smaller than in the major. That's to say that the distance between the two notes is shorter. The minor third sounds like this:

If you play these two examples one after the other, you should be able to hear a distinct difference between them. The first – the major – sounds bright, positive and cheerful, whereas the minor sounds slightly sadder and generally more downcast.

We can extend this premise so that it has an effect on different chords. If you play the two chords below, you should be able to hear the difference between them:

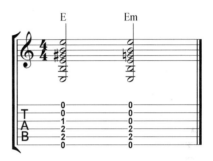

Both are E chords and look almost identical on the fretboard. In fact, I chose these two chords precisely because it's fairly easy to see that there's only one note's difference between them. Play them one after the other and really listen hard to spot the difference.

It might help you to come up with your own definition for what each type of chord sounds like. If, for instance, you think that a major chord sounds like a sunny day and the minor chord sounds like the threat of rain, so be it. The important thing is that you can tell the difference between the two, not how you do it. I don't care if you think that a major chord sounds like a red fire engine as long as the job gets done.

So, if you're going to go down the computer-based ear-training route, your first job should be to customise your program so that you can test yourself on recognising major and minor chords or *triads* (music-speak for a three-note basic major or minor chord) and don't move on until you're getting 100 per cent on the test every time. As with everything else in music, it's important not to rush on before you have the basic skills down pat. This is a lesson that forms an integral part of your core training as a musician and so it needs to be programmed in to the extent that it becomes an instinct and not a conscious choice every time.

Once you're confident in your ability to differentiate between major and minor chords, move on to the intervals that make up the major scale. Here's a little exercise that enables you to hear them one at a time against the root note of the scale:

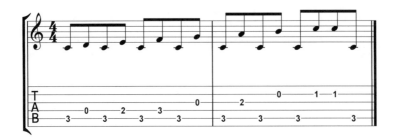

Here, it's a good idea to speak the name of each interval out loud as you play it – literally say aloud, 'Major second,' 'Major third,' and so on – as this will really make sure the information is embedded in your memory. (Incidentally, if you're at all self-conscious about talking to yourself as you practise, it might be a good idea to get over this as quickly as possible, because I'm going to ask you to sing in a minute...)

Repeat this exercise every day for a couple of minutes each time. There really is no better alternative to repetitive action when you're learning something like this. But make sure you don't make the common mistakes of repeating it too often at one sitting, carrying on for 20 minutes and believing that you don't need to do it any more for another week, or doing it for two minutes every day...for three days. Neither of these approaches is good for your ear training; only by doing this exercise little and often will you make a difference.

Once you've got the exercise under your fingers and can perform it fluently and with no mistakes, the next step is to hum, whistle or sing each note as you play it. You might feel like a total ass while you're doing this but, believe me, nothing works better than adding your own voice to something you're trying to learn. By making the sound of the intervals something that's being generated from within, you can increase your awareness of the lesson by an enormous amount. Seriously. I know I'm beginning to sound like a Zen master here, but I've been at this for 25 years and I know that it works. It's as simple as that.

Once again, if you're working with a computer program, set it up so that it plays random intervals from the major scale and then try to identify them as it plays them. As before, discipline yourself so that you don't move on until your score is continuously high.

You can practise this idea of randomising scale tones on the fretboard, too, like this:

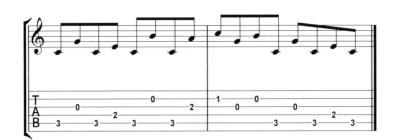

Playing this exercise is just one way of mixing up the notes of the major scale, and hopefully it'll give you enough of an idea to try out some of your own.

Next, if you've become quite adept at singing along with your playing, try singing the interval *before* you sound it on the guitar. Play the root note and then fret a random note from the scale but *don't pluck it* until you've had a go at singing it. You'll probably find that you're well off target

to begin with, but gradually you'll find yourself getting closer and closer to the right note.

You can extend this kind of idea to cover other areas of ear training, too. For instance, try the same sort of thing on a minor scale, like the one at the top of the next page.

Play some chords one note at a time and try to sing each note as you play it, until you've advanced to being able to sing each note *before* you play it.

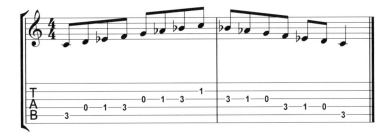

Try to work out melodies by humming them and finding the notes on the guitar fretboard. Don't try to be too ambitious too soon; start off with really well-known and ingrained melodies, such as nursery rhymes, folk songs and Christmas carols. Hum each one note at a time and keep humming each note while you find it on the guitar neck. You'll soon find that you can find the right note more and more quickly. This kind of exercise marks the start of the development of a serious level of musicianship and lays the groundwork for skills that will prove to be priceless in the future. A highly trained jazz musician can play what he hears in his head – indeed, it's the very heart of improvisation itself – and that journey begins with doing this kind of exercise.

Ear-training exercises can be fairly broad-based; basically, anything that increases your awareness of pitch and gives you an idea of how it relates directly to the guitar fretboard will be doing you a lot of good. As I said earlier, ear training is a part of learning music that's often overlooked, and yet it's an area where you can do an incredible amount of valuable work with just a little effort every day.

THE RIGHT APPROACH TO LEARNING CHORDS

When I hold seminars, I often ask my students how many chord shapes they think there are on the guitar. I usually get some answers that are obvious guesses, often quoting some astronomical figure and accompanied by a sort of *what-chance-have-we-got-to-learn-them-all?* type of shrug. It generally surprises them when I tell them that there are really only five.

You see, my question wasn't 'How many *chords* are there?'; it was 'How many chord *shapes* are there?' While the guitar is a very difficult instrument to play well, it makes up for this by enabling us to bypass a lot of the cruel activities endured by noviciates of other instruments and learn a lot of information by shape alone. Let me explain.

If you wanted to learn the saxophone instead of the guitar, you'd find that you'd be learning the same sort of information but in a very different way. For instance, you wouldn't need to bother about learning chords on a saxophone, as the sax can produce only one note at a time, but you'd need to learn *about* them and play their associated arpeggios. After all, as you'll see later, an arpeggio is really just a chord played one note at a time.

You'd also need to be aware of the general rationale of chord arrangements – how they work, what sort of implications there are for playing melodies above them and so on – so you'd concentrate on learning scales in order to become familiar with the physics of the instrument in general and, for the most part, you'd specialise in playing melody as opposed to accompaniment.

You'd also discover that every scale comes with a different fingering on the sax and that some scales are more problematic than others. Any obliging sax player will tell you that some keys are easier to play in than others; the key of B♭, for instance, is well known as being a very straightforward sax key, while sharp keys like E tend to be awkward. (Incidentally, if you've ever wondered why so many jazz tunes are written in B♭, it was to favour the horn players and give them an easy time of things!)

With the guitar, there are no such misfortunes. If we learn a scale or chord shape in one key, it's nearly always possible for us to transfer the same scale or chord in some form or other to all of the other keys with the absolute minimum effort. This goes some way to make up for the fact that we need to know all about chords, because, like it or not, we spend most of our time playing them.

So, where to begin? Well, I'm assuming that you've learned most of what I call the 'camp-fire collection' – that is, all the basic chords down at the guitar's nut, such as E, A, C, D and G major, along with E, A and D minor and a fistful of seventh chords on the side. If you haven't, this is where you should begin, as all of these chords are fairly easy to get your fingers around and don't involve too much in the way of big stretches or other digital athletics that take time to master. In fact, you can go a long way with just this basic starter pack of chord shapes, and indeed many players don't venture any further because they don't really experience the need.

I once gave lessons to a guy who was already an established professional on the local scene. He played in pubs and clubs as a soloist between five and seven nights a week and his repertoire consisted of Beatles songs and other timeless tunes from music's popular field. He was actually very good at what he did, and his gig sheet told me that he was in demand, but he came to me because he wanted to expand his knowledge of chords and open up his set to more adventurous material. It soon became clear to me, however, that he was very set in his ways and found it hard to assimilate the information I was giving him – particularly as it meant that he had to return to the basics in order to understand exactly what taking the next step forward really entailed. In the end, I told him I thought that in his case it was best to leave well alone and that he had little to gain by using more adventurous chords in the material he was performing, as if anything it would probably detract from what he was doing. After all, he was already earning a good living from playing music, so why fix something that wasn't broken? I think he was quite relieved to hear this, in fact. But his case was pretty much unique, in that expanding his knowledge base was actually working against him. It doesn't mean that you're off the hook!

Here's what I'd call a basic starter pack of chord shapes for the guitar:

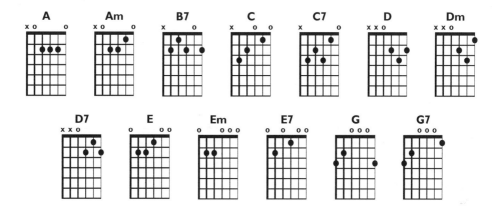

As you can see, there are three types of chord here, which I'm going to call the three basic *families* of chords: majors, minors and sevenths. None of them presents any real problems once your left hand is used to planting fingers on the fretboard.

The primary guidelines for playing chords are as follows:

Finger Position

As far as possible, the fingers on your left hand should always sit close to the back of frets, like this:

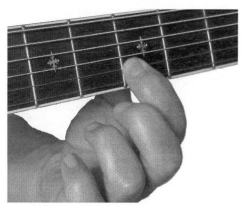

In order to get a clean note, the left-hand fingers need to be seated up against the back of the frets as far as possible

This position will give you the perfect 'lockoff' between fret and string. It isn't always possible for every chord – after all, rules are made to be broken – but it's still good general advice.

Thumb Position

This is critical. Many players – including those who have been playing for a while without the guidance of a teacher – often play with the thumb on their fretting hand in completely the wrong position and, as a result, find certain chords almost impossible to form. The most important rule here is that the thumb ought to be upright, as shown here, and not leaning to one side or the other:

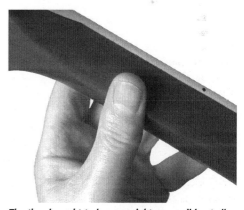

The thumb ought to be as upright as possible at all times so that it offers support to the fingers on the fretboard

With this kind of position, the thumb is supporting the fingers correctly and acting as a pivot. Indeed, you shouldn't have to grip the fretboard at all; instead, the aim is to eliminate all tension in your hands and arms, as a relaxed hand is far more flexible (and, medically speaking, happier) than one that's tensed up unnecessarily.

Buzz And Fluff

When you come across new or unfamiliar chords, play them one string at a time to make sure that you have a good clean note from each. However long you've been playing, it's likely that you'll encounter chords you've not seen before. When this happens, it's likely that you'll find the newcomer cumbersome or you might encounter some fingering difficulties, resulting in a couple of buzzy or indistinct notes. This is something that's easy to correct by altering the pressure of the fingers involved or by checking the thumb position to make sure that the fingers are all supported.

The most important thing here is to identify any potential problems and deal with them immediately by taking remedial action. Once again, don't leave these things to chance, telling yourself that minor fingering irregularities will magically disappear as you improve as a guitarist generally, as this isn't the case. The only way to deal with problems is to hit them head-on when you encounter them – and this will enable you to progress much faster.

Practise Sensibly

This won't be the last time I'll be giving you this advice in this book, but nevertheless it's a darned good idea to jot down a record of any problematic material you come across, using a book set aside for the purpose. I was introduced to this idea by a very wise classical guitar teacher named Bob Jones who encouraged his pupils to write down in one place everything they found difficult during their practice sessions and run through it all in isolation as part of their daily practice routines. For instance, they might have had trouble with a bar of music with some particularly tricky fingering, a chord change that called for some adept finger movement up or down the fretboard – whatever. The idea was that these potentially explosive parts of songs or pieces could all be successfully defused if they were isolated and practised separately.

In fact, I've proved the value of this lesson to myself several times – and not just in music, either. Occasionally I look back at pieces I was learning twenty years ago, and after a couple of plays through to reacquaint myself with the music I generally find that the difficult spots I didn't deal with properly or efficiently back then are still a problem for me today. The fact is that you can never expect to improve or progress on the guitar unless you deal with its more awkward moments as they occur, so keeping a record and disciplining yourself to play through each musical hairpin bend every time you practise is an excellent way to proceed. There are very few things that

can't be solved by simple repetition over a period of time, believe me.

Returning to the subject of establishing an order for learning chords, we've seen that there are essentially three families of chord types: major, minor and dominant seventh (often referred to as just 'sevenths'). Also, we've seen that there are 12 different notes in the musical scale:

A A♯/B♭ B C C♯/D♭ D D♯/E♭ E F F♯/G♭ G G♯/A♭
1   2   3 4 5   6   7   8 9 10   11 12

So, very simply put, it should be your aim to work towards knowing a major, minor and seventh chord for each of these 12 notes, giving you 36 chords in total. I fully realise that some chords occur more often than others in music, and that you might be thinking you're unlikely to use some of them, but you might be surprised at how often these supposedly unlikely candidates crop up in the most unusual places.

Also, if you've just picked up a chord book to seek out the missing chords from this repertoire I'm imposing upon you, you've probably found that some of the missing pieces have the most ungainly fingerings – which is probably why you've avoided them thus far. Fear not: there's an infallible system for learning all of them.

The Barre Facts

Realistically, the best way to learn chords is to learn to play *barre* versions as early as you possibly can. You've maybe found a couple of barre chords already, but for those unfamiliar with the term, a barre chord is one produced by laying a finger – usually the index finger – across the fretboard to stop all of the strings and then forming a chord above it (ie between that finger and the soundhole) using the remaining fingers on the left hand.

Here's an example of a very common barre shape:

And here's a picture to show you what's involved from a physical point of view:

An E major-shape barre chord

One thing you should notice is that the indents from the strings aren't along the 'face' of my finger but slightly to one side. So any book you might have read that tells you to 'lay your finger flat on the fingerboard' should now be consigned to the bin.

Your mission now is to find a good lockoff position for your index finger, and the first step here is a fairly obvious one: simply lay your finger down on the fingerboard as close as you can to the back of the fret (see the picture below) and play each string individually to make sure that you get a good clean sound from each:

Begin by laying the first finger across all six strings and playing them one by one to ensure you have all six notes ringing clearly

As you can see, here my first finger is laying over the fretboard while my remaining fingers form an E major-type shape.

To begin with, playing barre chords is going to feel like a tough proposition, physically, because they call for some considerable strength in the muscles controlling the index finger and thumb. In fact, you might have tried to play this type of chord before and found it almost impossible to hold for any longer than a few seconds, and this is entirely normal. There are a few things that are impossible to speed up where playing is concerned, and muscle development is at the top of the list. Even the most impatient guitar student can't expect a biological process like the growing of muscle tissue to occur overnight; all you can do is practise regularly, patiently and repetitively and wait for the physical exercise to do its work. So, if you're someone who has said in the past, 'I can't play barre chords,' ask yourself this: Have you ever *really* worked on them?

One of the most common causes of problems encountered while playing barre chords is poor finger position. The picture below clearly shows the indents in my finger after playing a barre (and after pressing my finger into the strings hard enough to make a good picture – the things I do for art, etc).

If you don't get a completely clean tone – and it's very common to find one or two notes that go *plop* at first instead of producing a clear note – then take a good look at what's going on physically with your finger. Have any of the strings got themselves under the natural grooves in your fingers (ie where the joints are)? Is your thumb doing its job of supporting the fingers correctly?

Have patience if things don't go well initially. You might simply need to wait and practise until your finger muscles have developed sufficiently.

Once you have a full set of six ringing strings under your barre, it's time to move on and form some simple shapes with the rest of your fingers:

These are indentations that the strings have made on my first finger after playing a barre chord. You'll notice that the grooves are towards the side of the finger rather than on the flat part

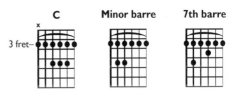

C   Minor barre   7th barre

3 fret—

The three simple shapes on the previous page are all built around the E-type chord down at the nut. With barres, the rules for forming the chords are just as they are for any other type of chord: try to ensure a good lock between fret and string, play each string one at a time and make any necessary adjustments immediately.

However adept you are at forming barres in the early days, you'll still be able to hold them down for only a short period of time until nature provides you with the vice-like grip necessary to endure a 90-minute barre-based set on stage. So I'm asking you once again to remain patient while this happens. Don't fret about it (pardon the pun); just practise your barres regularly and all will be well.

It's quite natural to experience discomfort in your left hand – especially between the forefinger and thumb – while you get it up to barring speed; you might find yourself suffering from varying degrees of cramp-like pain in the hand, for instance. If this happens, stop and rest for a few moments; you're not training for the Marines here, so there's no need to put yourself through torture just so you can play barre chords. The 'no pain, no gain' adage is all well and good, but it's definitely not applicable here; pain in the hand is sometimes indicative of something going wrong, and if it persists then it's time to consult a medical professional. There's more advice on how to avoid guitar-related health problems in the section 'An Apple A Day', in the 'Introduction' to Part 2, but for now let's practise safe barres, OK?

So why am I putting so much emphasis on barre-chord shapes? You remember I said that there are really only five shapes for forming chords on the guitar? Well, nearly all of them rely on a good basic barre-chord technique.

To begin at the beginning, cast your mind back to the days when you were first learning chords down at the nut end of the fretboard. You would have come across shapes for C major, A major, G major, E major and D major fairly early on – in other words, these shapes here:

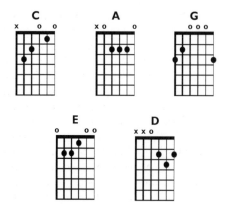

Nothing controversial about any of them; they're just basic, easy-to-play shapes that are to be found in thousands of different songs.

Now, the nature of the guitar – the way it's tuned and so on – means that shapes tend to repeat all over the place. The simplest barre shapes prove this; for instance, new students generally meet these two first of all:

These two chords are barred versions of the shapes you'd play for E and A major respectively:

The other shapes I mentioned – C, G and D major – are generally not thought of as being terribly practical in terms of actual barre chords, but that doesn't mean they're not moveable. After all, anything that works for the E and A shapes has to work for the other three, right? So, even though these other three shapes can sometimes be a little more awkward to manoeuvre, they can still be useful in much the same way as E and A are.

Now, believe it or not, these five chord shapes (which, incidentally, are easy to remember because they spell the word CAGED) are the five 'master' chord shapes on the fretboard, and nearly every other chord you can play on the guitar is based on them. So, obviously, learning where they all fall in any key would form the beginnings of a pretty powerful system for becoming familiar with the whole fretboard.

To see better how this principle works, let's look at the key of C major and find out where all the CAGED shapes fall. The first is pretty obvious; it's the one we started with, down at the nut:

The next time we come across a chord shape for C, it's a barre position at the third fret:

Here we have the A shape once again, but at this position it actually gives us another version of C major. I'll explain why a little later, but for now just trust me!

If you move another few frets up the guitar neck, you'll come across this position:

Now, I'll be the first to say that this is one awkward chord shape to play in this form, so don't hurt yourself trying to finger it just yet; just be aware that this is where the G shape for C major is positioned on your guitar.

The next version of C major crops up at the eighth fret and will probably look familiar:

It's the E-shape barre chord for C.

The next one isn't a full barre as such, but if you take a good look at it you'll find that it's nothing more scary-looking than an ordinary D-shape chord played at the tenth fret:

So now we have five basic shapes for C major up the fretboard – and that's it; we're done with that chord. Just to prove it, take a look at what happens if you move up another few frets and make a barre at the 12th fret:

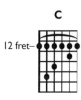

By the time you get to this chord, you've worked your way back to the basic C shape once again, and if you go on into the twilight zone at the top of the neck (known in guitar circles as 'the dusty end') you'll find that the other shapes all repeat in the same order, too.

So, to recap, in the key of C major there are five basic chord shapes that span the entire fretboard and spell out the word 'CAGED' as they do so.

Now, this isn't just a coincidence, something that just happens and isn't particularly worth mentioning; the *CAGED system*, as it's known, is in fact the starting point from which you can organise the entire fretboard, learn loads of chord shapes and put these shapes together with scales, too. In other words, it's an incredibly worthwhile system to learn. It's used by many guitar players, and once upon a time it was one of the best kept secrets of guitar playing. I personally learned about it from the late jazz guitar genius Joe Pass, with whom I attended a seminar back in the early '80s. When I left the theatre where the seminar was being held that afternoon, my head was full of ideas and I rushed home and wrote down everything I could remember in case I forgot it later. The rest I worked out for myself over time, and I still call upon the CAGED system from time to time, even today.

If you want proof that all these shapes are in fact alternatives for the C major chord we know and love at the bottom of the fretboard, here goes...

In music, any major or minor chord is basically three notes – nothing more. These groups of three notes are known as *triads*, the *tri* bit being from the Latin *tres* or Greek *treis* and meaning, not surprisingly, 'three'. But you don't really need to know that; just drop it into the conversation next time you're talking to someone about music to look clever. Anyway, as far as C major is concerned, these three notes are C, E and G, which are all members of the C major scale – the first, third and fifth members, respectively, in fact:

C D (E) F (G) A B C
1 2 (3) 4 (5) 6 7 1

If you're curious about how it came about that these three notes in particular were chosen to represent the key of C harmonically, it was something that was sorted out around 400 years ago, and these notes were chosen probably just because they sounded good. If you're at all in doubt about this, try putting some of the other notes from the scale together and see what you can come up with. You'll probably agree that these three give you the 'vanilla' sound of C major whereas everything else begins to sound a little 'tutti frutti'.

So, as we're talking about just three notes, let's examine which ones make up the five shapes in the key of C.

To begin with, the first position or 'nut' position gives us these notes from bottom to top:

C E G C E

On to the third-position barre:

This chord gives us these notes, from bass to treble:

C G C E G

They're the same notes but mixed up in a slightly different order. Play them one after the other and you might be able to tell a difference.

On to the G-shape position now:

This particular shape yields these notes:

C E G C E C

It's another mix of those same three notes, with nothing added or taken away.

Then, at the eighth fret, we meet the most familiar barre shape for C:

This time, the three-note mix is as follows:

C G C E G C

And lastly, this little D shape crops up at the tenth fret:

It's a four-note chord comprising these notes:

C G C E

So there you have it: the whole fretboard covered with those three notes that make up the chord of C major.

Now, if you think about it, we've probably incorporated all the Cs, Es and Gs that there are on the fretboard, taking into account that they have to be reachable by the average human hand. In other words, that's why these shapes can be thought of as the 'masters'. Even if you can find some other shapes on the fretboard for C major, they'll no doubt be related to one of the CAGED shapes we've already covered in one way or another. In fact, the way to advance your learning of chords is to teach yourself to pick out these relationships – and we'll be doing a little of that in a minute.

While we're here, though, I should say a few words about the mix of notes you can get away with using within a chord. As you can see from the above, we're dealing with only three notes; they're just present in the different shapes in varying proportions. So what's the difference? Why do we need to know more than one shape for any chord?

Well, you've no doubt heard about variety being the spice of life, and this is certainly true in music. The five shapes we've looked at for C major might all contain the same notes, but you've probably noticed that they all sound different to one another. This is all down to the mix of those three basic chord tones. Take, for instance, these two:

C E G C E

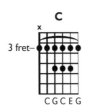

C G C E G

Both of these chords are formed down at the nut end, so they're drawing from the same basic supply of Cs, Es and Gs on offer. But if that's the case, why do they sound a bit different in tone to one another?

The reason for this is all down to the way in which the various notes are repeated within the chord shape. The first shape has two Cs, one G and two Es, whereas the second has two Cs, two Gs and one E. Not much of a difference, you might think, and you'd be right, but it's nevertheless enough to affect the basic timbre of the chord. (Remember that *timbre* just means the quality of the sound, as opposed to its pitch.) This means that not only do you have a choice of position for playing a C major chord but you also have some control over how it sounds, which can prove an invaluable resource if you ever need to arrange a song for guitar. Loosely speaking, if one version of C

doesn't quite fit the bill, try a couple of others and see if they're any closer to what you're looking for. Just think of the alternatives as being actually the same chord but with different hairstyles, or the same car but in different colours – anything that helps you to visualise exactly what's going on. The fact that different *voicings* of chords can sound quite different to one another is a general rule, and it's quite an important one to come to terms with early on.

The reason behind this difference in timbre between chords of the same basic name lies in the quality of the intervals concerned. When triads are stripped down to their basics, they comprise two interval-to-root relationships: one between the first and third in the chord...

C–E

...and the other between the root and fifth:

C–G

Play each of these component parts one after the other and listen closely. How do they sound to you? How would you categorise them in order to be able to tell them apart?

A common system is to categorise the third as sounding sweet and the fifth as savoury. (It's a well-known fact that adding thirds to a chord makes it sound sweeter, whereas adding fifths makes it sound stronger and more rock 'n' roll.) In less enlightened times, the major third used to be known as the *feminine interval* (I'm not kidding) and the fifth was referred to as *masculine*. I'm sure you don't need me to tell you why this form of reference isn't in use today.

So this is the reason why the E- and A-shape barre chords tend to be used for rock accompaniment, whereas the C and G shapes are used in more balladic contexts. Of course, this isn't a hard-and-fast rule and is wide open to question, but I thought I'd point it out here, if only to introduce you to the different kinds of textures available to you with these chords.

So, now you've seen how C major chords can be planted in order, up and down the guitar fretboard, and how they form a kind of structure at the same time. But what if you want a major chord other than C? What happens then?

Well, the good news is that the CAGED system works in *every* key. It doesn't matter if you want to play in E♭, G♯, F, A♭ or E; the order of the chords going up the fretboard will always spell the word CAGED if you use this system. So maybe now you're beginning to see why this is such a popular system for mapping out the fretboard; learn it once and you can then apply it to all 12 major keys. Of course, the chords all move around a bit in the various keys, but the order of the shapes is always the same: C, A, G, E and D. So the next step is to learn how to establish some landmarks.

Let's look once again at the five CAGED shapes:

Here's the C shape once again, but this time there's a line pointing to its lowest note, the root of the chord and the note that gives the chord its name. In the diagram above, the note is C, but move the whole shape up two frets and hey presto! It becomes a barre for D major:

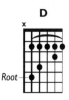

And if we move it up another couple of frets, it becomes E major:

The logic here is very simple: if a chord sounds right in one position, it will sound just as good in another, as long as there aren't any stray open strings left ringing to spoil things. All you need is a system for finding its shape and you've actually learned 12 chords at once. Useful? I think so!

So, your next step is to create a neck diagram that lists the notes on the sixth, fifth and fourth strings. I encourage you to do this yourself because I want to invoke what's often termed *pen memory*, whereby you're more likely to remember something if you write it out. Also, you should make your diagram as large as possible – an A3-sized piece of paper would be ideal, for instance – so that you can refer to it while you're holding your guitar. Any smaller than A3 and you'll probably have to put the guitar down and pore over it, thus breaking the continuity of the exercise I'm going to recommend shortly.

Basically, you should end up with a larger version of this:

Don't just copy mine; instead, work out the order of the notes on the strings for yourself as an exercise and refer back to the diagram above to make sure that you're on target.

You'll notice that this diagram contains only the *whole notes* – ie, not the flats and sharps. I've omitted these in the interests of clarity; you can maybe imagine how cluttered things would become if there was an A♯/B♭ squeezed in between the A and B, etc. As far as the positioning of the sharps and flats goes, just remember this:

Flat is one fret to the left of any given note and sharp is one fret to the right

With this in mind, if you know that the note G is on the third fret, bass E string, you should be able to work out easily where G♭ and G♯ hang out, yes? Good. So, instead of cluttering it up, keep your diagram as clear as possible and get on with some note-spotting.

Study your own neck diagram and you should see the simple logic behind moving the C-shape barre around the fretboard. Down at the nut, the note at the root (third fret, A string) is very clearly a C. Move it up one fret at a time and it becomes C♯, D, D♯, E, etc, in turn. So one barre ultimately gives you 12 chords.

Now let's look at where the root notes are for all of the other CAGED shapes:

A shape

G shape

E shape

D shape

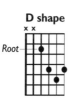

The E and G shapes take their names from notes on the sixth string, the A and C shapes from notes on the fifth and the D shape from a note on the fourth. Spend a while doing some simple orienteering, taking any of the shapes shown here, moving it around on the fretboard (using your neck diagram as a guide) and trying it out against a chord shape you know. For instance, if you take the E shape and try to find a D major chord, when you think you've found it, check it with the 'camp-fire D' down at the nut:

D

D

This cross-checking should keep you on track as you familiarise yourself with the CAGED system.

The next thing to do is practise working with the CAGED system every day. Here's a brief guide to the best way to proceed:

- Pick any note at random. Find the lowest version of that note on your diagram. It will usually (although not necessarily always) be on the bass string.

- Play the corresponding barre shape for that chord.

- Work out the next shape up the fretboard. If the first shape that presents itself to you is a G shape, you know that the next shape up must be an E. Just remember that the sequence always spells out the word 'CAGED'.

- Now find the next shape, and the next, and so on until you've covered all five shapes.

- The next day, do the same thing, following the same rules but starting from a different note.

This might sound like a laborious method of learning the system, and it certainly involves a lot of foundation-digging to begin with, but it *will* give you an enormous advantage when you come to extend your knowledge of chords.

With my private students, I'd spend the first ten minutes or so of an hour-long lesson focusing on exercises, and one of the staples was finding the CAGED chords in a key of my choice. As you'll see in the 'Scales' chapter, you can expand the CAGED system so that it relates to scale positions, too, which ultimately makes it a priceless tool for navigating around the guitar neck.

Keep the above exercise as part of your daily routine (along with the workout in Part 2!) until you can find all the chords in any given key instantly. Even then, the chances are that you'll need to review it occasionally, so when you think you know what you're doing just come back to it once a week or so to keep sharp.

So much for the major chords. What about the rest of them? OK, this is where things become really interesting.

Take a look at these chord boxes:

Major shape

Minor shape

7th shape

Here are three chords that we've seen before, and you've probably spotted that all are variations of the CAGED E shape. You can turn the major shape into a minor one by removing one finger, and you can turn it into a seventh shape by removing another. In other words, here are three E-shape variations that can be turned instantly into 36 chords simply by applying the barre-chord rule of moving things around the neck. That's three chords for each of the 12 degrees of the chromatic scale, giving 36 chords in total.

Here, it's important to gain the ability to connect the chord shapes you come across with those of the CAGED system, as this will speed up your learning of chords considerably and will aid you in mapping out the whole fretboard. It's much more helpful to block off the fretboard into five specific areas and work on these independently than to approach the fretboard as being one long and mysterious plank of wood.

Here's an example of this 'relationship' business in action:

F

You'll recognise this as an F major chord, one of the fingering hurdles you come across first of all when you start working through a chord book. Now take a look at this:

F

All I've done here is fill in the lower two strings. You should be able to see straight away that this is a pruned-down version of an E-shape barre and is therefore quite easy to categorise, to move up the fretboard and to remember as 12 separate major chords.

Obviously, I won't be exploring the CAGED system of chord production too much further because the topic would need a whole book to be covered completely. Before I move on, though, here's a couple of examples of the next stage.

After recognising chord fragments like the F chord above and relating it to its parental home, the next step is to learn to spot things like this:

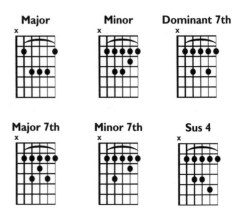

Major   Minor   Dominant 7th

Major 7th   Minor 7th   Sus 4

Here's an A-shape major barre accompanied by some of its offspring – a minor, a dominant seventh, a major seventh, a minor seventh and a sus4 – that have all been created through the simple act of moving a finger or two from the parent A barre. If you've applied the 12-chords-at-a-time rule I explained earlier here, you've just learned 72 chords!

The basic skill here is one of *visualisation*, which for a guitarist is a very important one to develop. You need to gain the ability to be able to see these things and visualise what's happening within any given shape, as doing so will accelerate your rate of learning tenfold.

Here's an exercise that will help you in this regard. Pick up any chord book and try to relate the shapes you see in it to one of the five master versions. I used to get my private students to do this, and after a while they would stop asking me to tell them the shapes of each chord.

Alternatively, convert each of the five shapes into as many variants as possible. Just think about what happens when you play a G7 chord instead of a G major. There's just one finger-change different between the two:

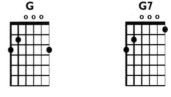

G   G7

Now apply this technique to forming chords up the rest of the neck. Obviously barring a G7 isn't going to be easy, but when you come across this kind of problem remember the idea of chord fragments. In this case, we could easily prune the G7 barre down to this:

This is a perfectly usable seventh-type chord, derived from the G-shape barre in the CAGED system. Once you're used to visualising where the G shape falls in any key, you shouldn't have trouble finding this particular shape anywhere on the fretboard.

What's In A Name?

While we're on the subject, it's probably a good idea for me to include a few words here about where all the different chord names come from. If you've browsed through a chord book, you've almost certainly noticed the rich variety of chord names on offer and been somewhat daunted by the prospect of learning even a small fraction of them. But there's a shortcut to learn here, too; what you need to do is rationalise all these different names and types and develop a system for learning them.

You've already seen that there are really only five master shapes, from which all other shapes are derived, even if some of them have only the faintest family resemblance to their parents. And, as I mentioned earlier, there are only three basic family groups: majors, minors and sevenths. The next step is to put everything together. But how? The answer to this question lies in studying how chords are formed – and it's really a lot less complicated than you might think.

Music convention dictates that chords are formed from two octaves of a scale, so let's take a close look at the C major scale:

C D E F G A B C D E F G A B C
1 2 3 4 5 6 7 1 9 3 11 5 13 7 1

Don't worry; I haven't forgotten how to count past seven. This is just music's way of confusing things. If we break this system down, you'll see that the first octave of the scale is numbered 1–7:

C D E F G A B C
1 2 3 4 5 6 7 1

The number 1 on the right represents where the second octave starts, and C will always be known as the root or '1' of its own scale. But from there, things get a little wacky.

For a start, all of the even numbers have disappeared and been substituted with odd ones. What's going on there?

C D E F G A B C
1 9 3 11 5 13 7 1

Well, remember when we were looking at triads earlier? I mentioned then that chords are made up from the first, third and fifth notes of a scale, like this:

C major = C E G
1 3 5

Let's say I wanted to add the note D to that triad and turn it into a four-note chord:

C D E G
1 2 3 5

The fact that the note D is only a couple of frets away from C and the same distance from E is going to make things sound very cluttered indeed. This is a shame because the note D can actually add a lot to this particular triad – but only if the distance between it and the basic triad is increased. So, in most guitar voicings of this chord, you'll see the D added in such a way that it's kept separate from its neighbours in order to avoid producing an ear-jarring clash. In order to make this positioning absolutely clear in the chord name, the number 9 is used instead of 2, indicating that the D is, in fact, in the upper octave.

Have a go at playing this so you can hear what kind of difference this repositioning makes:

C with D added   **C add 9**

Playing the first chord gives you the chance to hear what the D sounds like when it's left in close proximity to the C, while the second has the D in it but at a safe distance from any possible clash. Better? (You'll see why the chord is called 'C add 9' in a minute or two.) It really is as simple as that; the names of most chords are merely shorthand references to the notes that they contain. Let's take a look at some other examples and I'll show you what I mean.

Cmaj7

OK, this is derived from a major chord, so we know it already contains the first, third and fifth of its major scale:

C E G
1 3 5

Now here's the breakdown of a Cmaj7:

C E G B
1 3 5 7

The number 7 here indicates which member of the scale has been added to give it a bit of seasoning. In the case of C major, the seventh is a B...

C D E F G A (B) C
1 2 3 4 5 6 (7) 1

...and if it's added to a C major chord, here's what you get:

C E G B

So what about C6? Let's do the maths:

C + E + G + the sixth note of the C scale = C E G A
1 3 5   1 3 5 6

Things become a little less clear when we get to chords like Cmaj9, though. In this case, it's true that the basic 1, 3 and 5 are still present in the chord, but it also contains both the seventh and ninth degrees of the scale:

C E G B D
1 3 5 7 9

Why this anomaly? Once again, it's down to a set of rules that have been present in music for hundreds of years and which really aren't worth worrying about. They do add another layer of confusion to an already nebulous subject, true, but I'm sure you'll cope.

So it's possible to go on adding notes of the major scale to the basic triad and coming up with many different-sounding chords. Here are a few more:

Cmaj: C E G
Cmaj6: C E G A
Cmaj7: C E G B
Cadd9: C E G D*
Cmaj9: C E G B D
C6/9: C E G A B

The only other bump in the road, as far as chord logic is concerned, is with the fourth note of the scale – in the case of C major, the F. You know the saying, 'There's always one, isn't there?' Well, if ever there was a note that totally screws everything up, it's the fourth. It's so close to the third and fifth that it tends to make everything sound rather nasty. Even putting it up an octave only really half works, as you'll notice if you play this:

C E G C F

So the solution is to omit the third from the chord so that it's possible to make use of the fourth's unique characteristics:

Csus4

And because we've taken some fairly unusual steps in that we've broken the original triad apart, the chord gets a special name: 'sus 4' or 'suspended fourth'. When it's written down in letters and numbers, it looks like this:

C F G
1 4 5

At the top of the next page are a few more suspended chords. Play through a few of them, resolving them into their major triads (ie Dsus4 to Dmaj) and listen to what they sound like.

* This is why the C chord with just the extra D in it is called 'Cadd9' instead of 'Cmaj9'. They are, in fact, different chords.

Asus4
x o   o

Dsus4
x x o

Esus4
o   o o

You'll notice that it has four different notes, whereas the major chord has just three. The extra note is the flat seventh – ie the regular seventh degree of the C major scale (B) that has been 'flattened' or reduced in pitch by a semitone – and it's this note that gives the chord its name. Play these two chords, C and C7, and listen closely to hear how they sound different:

C
x   o   o

C7
x   o

You'll very probably decide that you've heard this sort of sound a lot in the past, and you'd probably be right, as it's by far the most common use of suspended chords.

So now you should have a pretty good idea about how chords are named and why. Musically speaking, the other scale tones present in each chord slightly change what's commonly referred to as its *colour* or *texture*. Just as you listened hard to the various mixes of basic triad tones a while back, spend some time with a chord book and really listen hard to the difference between the straight major and, say, the same chord with an added ninth or major sixth. In most cases, chords like sixths, major ninths and major sevenths are interchangeable with straight major chords, so gaining a thorough understanding of this system of chord naming and production will add considerably to your powers as a musician – for instance, enabling you to arrange tunes so that they sound more interesting.

Years ago, the straight major chords were known as 'vanilla' chords, due to the fact that they're very simple and sound rather tired and ordinary to most musicians' jaded ears. For this reason, many musicians – notably those in the jazz fraternity – would add tones to them to make them more colourful. This is a simple and yet very effective device for arranging even the most straightforward tune creatively.

But meanwhile, what about the other two chord families, the minors and dominants? You'll be glad – and even a little relieved – to know that the same device can be applied to both of these chord groups. Take a look at this C dominant scale:

C   D   E   F   G   A   B♭   C
1   2   3   4   5   6   7   1

Note that the dominant scale differs from the major by only one degree: the seventh, which is 'flattened' to leave a whole-tone gap at the top of the scale. The reasoning behind this is explained later in chapter on 'Scales', but for now just be aware of this fundamental difference.

In any case, the basic form of the dominant-seventh chord looks like this:

C   E   G   B♭
1   3   5   ♭7

You'll probably agree that the ordinary major chord sounds rested and final, whereas the dominant chord sounds like it badly needs to go somewhere else, that its work is unfinished. The place it needs to go, in fact, is its key centre or root chord, like this:

C7
x   o

F
x x

Here, the C7 chord followed by one of F major sounds like a good end to a musical sentence; you get the impression of this serving as a full stop rather than as, say, a comma. Loosely speaking, this is indeed the function of a dominant chord: to signpost the ear towards the root or home chord. In order to hear it at work in context, try playing this example:

| C / / / | F / / / | G / / / | C / / / |

Now play this:

| C / / / | F / / / | G7 / / / | C / / / |

You should be able to hear that the second example gives a clear aural signpost back to the C when you reach the G7 chord. The first example, meanwhile, has an ordinary G major chord instead and so doesn't really deliver the same results, despite being absolutely correct, musically speaking.

I'm not going to go into too much detail about chord theory here, but you should be aware of the basic rules involved as they'll serve you well in your pursuit of a fuller understanding of how everything works in music.

These 'musical signpost' seventh chords crop up quite often in every type of song, irrespective of style; you'll find them in pop, rock, classical, skateboard punk – everywhere, in fact. We're not just stuck with the simple four-note variety, either; sevenths offer the biggest variety of different flavours available in the chord world.

Next, take a look at two octaves of the dominant scale:

C	D	E	F	G	A	B♭	C	D	E	F	G	A	B♭	C
1	2	3	4	5	6	7	1	9	3	11	5	13	7	1

You'll notice that the rather wacky system of numbering is used for this scale, too, and that only odd numbers are used after the initial seven.

So, given that a basic seventh chord looks like this...

$$C7: \quad C \quad E \quad G \quad B♭$$

...that means it's possible to add to it exactly as we did earlier with a straight triad in order to introduce different nuances to the basic seventh sound. Here are a few examples:

$$C9: \quad C \quad E \quad G \quad B♭ \quad D$$
$$C11: \quad C \quad E \quad G \quad B♭ \quad F$$
$$C13: \quad C \quad E \quad G \quad B♭ \quad D \quad A$$

Notice that the C11 chord contains the party-pooper note, F. Once again, it will clash with the third, but for some reason it doesn't sound quite as bad in this chord as it does in major chords – depending, of course, on what voicing you choose.

That's not the end of the story as far as seventh chords are concerned, either. As well as other scale tones, you'll quite likely come across some dominant chords that incluce chromatic tones to provide colour too. These chromatic tones are non-scale tones, visitors from outside the key that add dissonance, or musical 'seasoning', to a chord, quite literally spicing it up. The most common *altered seventh*, as this family of chords is called, is the 7♯9, known variously as the 'sharp nine' or 'sharpened ninth' chord. It looks like this:

C7♯9

You might recognise it as being part of the language of the blues and from being a staple in Jimi Hendrix's chord vocabulary. Its vital parts look like this:

$$C7♯9: \quad C \quad E \quad G \quad B♭ \quad D♯$$
$$ \quad 1 \quad 3 \quad 5 \quad ♭7 \quad ♯9$$

Here the ninth of the chord has simply been sharpened by a semitone (ie moved up one fret). Compare it to an ordinary ninth and you'll hear what I mean about it serving as a kind of musical spice:

C9

Here's another example of how important it is to be able to visualise what's going on where chord and scale shapes are concerned. It's obvious that the two chords are different, and yet it's fairly easy to see exactly *how* they're different and *why*. Many novice guitar players would see these as two separate chords, but actually seeing them as variations on one shape makes them far easier to learn.

Just as the naming of majors and sevenths employs a sort of musical shorthand to explain how their basic ingredients have been added to, minor chords follow suit in the exact same way. Well, nearly the same...

If you've already glanced through the chapter on 'Scales' (I realise that you're not necessarily reading this book in order), you'll have seen that the subject of minor scales isn't quite as clear as that of majors and sevenths. In general terms, the same rules for spicing up minor chords apply, in that you can take a basic minor scale like the one shown below and use it to add tones to a basic minor triad, as before. However, the world of minor scales isn't quite as cut and dried as that of major scales, so sometimes you'll see minor chords with very odd-looking additions indeed.

In this instance, I've employed both the notes A and A♭ as the sixth in the minor scale. The reasoning here is that the A♭ is actually textbook correct, but it's the A♮ (or *natural*) that you'll find in Cm6 chords. See what I mean about minor chords being not as straightforward as their major counterparts?

C	D	E♭	F	G	A/A♭	B♭	C	D	E♭	F	G	A/A♭	B♭	C
1	2	3	4	5	6	7	1	9	3	11	5	13	7	1

So some common minor chord forms would be these:

Cm: C E♭ G
Cm6: C E♭ G A
Cm7: C E♭ G B♭
Cm9: C E♭ G B♭ D

Although there seem to be some anomalies at work here – and there are doubtless things about all this heavy-duty theory that you don't yet fully understand – my advice is not to worry about them too much. Music works in mysterious ways, as you've no doubt already suspected, and none of us knows all the answers to every one of its weird twists and turns. The important thing is to be able to recognise some fundamentals, as follows:

• There are basically three chord families.

• All chord shapes are basically variations of five master shapes.

• Chord names are basically shorthand for each chord's contents.

• Chord extensions are used to add colour and texture to an accompaniment.

Everything else can wait – for now, at least. If you feel the need to delve further into music's mysterious inner core, there's a wealth of information available on the internet (some of it's even accurate) and a whole library's worth of books out there that will help you in your search. For now, though, just leave the more arcane aspects of music well alone and concentrate on the fundamentals.

One more thing before we leave the subject of chords. You might have come across two more chord types, *diminished* and *augmented*, on your travels and be wondering exactly where they fit in to the general plan. In fact, both of these types occur naturally in music harmony – in other words, they are entirely necessary to the general flow of things. It's the push-and-pull, dark-and-light, sweet-and-sour contrasts in music that keep it interesting. Sometimes chords that sound dissonant are added to an arrangement in order to act as an opposing musical force to the sweet-sounding stuff. Again, it's just like adding spice to a sauce: in moderation, it works perfectly, but if you overdo it, you're in trouble.

I make this point to prepare you for the way in which both diminished and augmented chords sound. Neither is what you might call pretty but, as I say, they're there for a purpose. So here they are:

C augmented
x x x

C E G♯

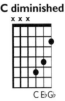

C diminished
x x x

C E♭G♭

Don't worry, the sound will grow on you. Before we get to grips with these two weird-sounding interlopers, though, let's look at where they fit into the general chordal hierarchy.

We've seen that there are three basic chord families – majors, minors and sevenths – and most people file these two with sevenths, more because of the way in which they're used in music than due to their actual construction.

Let's take a look at the augmented chord first. C augmented's basic triad is made up like this:

C E G♯
1 3 ♯5

You should be able to see straight away that it looks like a major chord gone horribly wrong. If not, here's a C major and C augmented chord together:

Major: C E G
        1 3 5

Aug: C E G♯
      1 3 ♯5

As you can see, in the latter example the fifth in the triad has been sharpened – or *augmented* – by a semitone to give it a restless, urgent, dissonant sound. The reason why the augmented chord is a sort of honorary member of the dominant-seventh family is because you're more likely to meet it in the guise of an augmented-seventh chord, like the one below, rather than in its basic triadic form:

Caug7
x x

8 fret—

This chord always puts me in the mind of rock 'n' roll; it's the first sound you hear on Chuck Berry's 'No Particular Place To Go', for instance, whereas the triadic version occurs at the beginning of The Beatles' 'Oh, Darlin''. (Incidentally, it's good to be able to file away sounds in this way for future reference. Associating chords with the songs in which they occur is a very good way of remembering them.)

On to the diminished chord now, which is constructed like this:

C   E♭   G♭

Once again, we're messing with the basic triad, and this time it's the turn of the minor triad to have its fifth altered:

$$\begin{array}{lccc} \text{Cm:} & C & E♭ & G \\ & 1 & ♭3 & 5 \end{array}$$

$$\begin{array}{lccc} \text{Cdim:} & C & E♭ & G♭ \\ & 1 & ♭3 & ♭5 \end{array}$$

Whereas an augmented chord comprises a *major* triad with an altered fifth, the diminished triad is made up of a *minor* triad with an altered fifth. And the way in which it's been altered is different, too; in the diminished triad the fifth has been flattened by one degree, hence its name.

Like the augmented, you're more likely to find the diminished chord occurring in the guise of a diminished seventh, which is what gives it the right to be treated as an honorary member of the family of sevenths:

Cdim7

There's one odd thing about both of these chords that comes to light when you look at their roots. Ordinarily, it's possible to find the root of any chord shape and then move it around the fretboard to all the various keys by lining it up with different roots along the string. With the augmented chord, however, *each note* of the basic triad can act as a root. This concept's a bit of a headbuster to begin with, for sure, but if you think about it, it actually makes things simpler.

Let's take another look at the C augmented triad:

C aug: C   E   G♯

Because all of the intervals in the triad are the same distance apart – in other words, it's what you might call a

symmetrical chord – if you started playing it from the second and third notes, you'd end up with the E augmented and G♯ augmented.

$$\begin{array}{lccc} \text{E aug:} & E & G♯ & C \\ \text{G♯ aug:} & G♯ & C & E \end{array}$$

If you play these two one after the other, you'll hear that they sound similar and yet completely different at the same time:

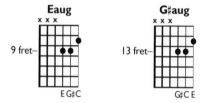

This is actually quite handy, because it means you need to memorise only one shape, from which you can then play three different chords. Economical, eh?

The same is actually true of the diminished chord: its component parts are the same distance from each other, so one basic shape gives you a bunch of chords.

$$\begin{array}{lcccc} \text{Cdim7:} & C & E♭ & G♭ & A \\ \text{E♭dim7:} & E♭ & G♭ & A & C \\ \text{G♭dim7:} & G♭ & A & C & E♭ \\ \text{Adim7:} & A & C & E♭ & G♭ \end{array}$$

Take a listen:

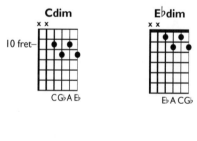

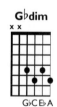

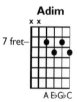

Once again, these sound like four different chords that are all strangely related somehow – and now you know why that is. Thus ends another lesson in economical shape learning: four chords from one.

We've covered quite a lot of ground since I first revealed to you that there are only five basic chord shapes, and this chapter probably represents an awful lot of work for you if you decide to take things to their logical conclusion. If you do, though, be aware that music harmony – which is basically what we're talking about here – gets even weirder the more you explore it, but fear not: all the information you'll need can be found in libraries, the internet and magazines if you decide to make the journey in full.

SONGS AND CHORD ARRANGEMENTS

Many players take their first steps into the world of playing songs with a sense of bewilderment. After all, there are so many songs; no one can remember them all, surely? Well, no, perhaps not. For this reason, most music students are very pleasantly surprised when they realise that songs are usually written to a basic formula and that learning a few simple rules makes the job a whole lot easier.

It would be awful if songs were just random collections of chords with melodies strung over them, with absolutely no sense of order or shape. In fact, if this was the case, such songs would probably be considered far too abstract to enjoy. Ever since the popular song as we know it today began its long, slow evolution, songwriters have been using tried and tested formulae for their work, giving the listener a sense of immediate familiarity on the one hand and something new to listen to on the other.

Of course, just because there's a formula at work doesn't mean that every song is going to sound the same – indeed, far from it. If you think about it, a whole street full of houses can look completely different in terms of design and décor, and yet they'll all have roofs, walls, windows, doors, etc, in very similar and predictable configurations.

The same can be said of songs. For instance, one of the fundamental blueprints for song design is what's known as *verse–chorus order*. For the last 100 years or so,* a great many songs have been built to this structure:

Verse   Verse   Chorus   Verse

Pieces constructed to this pattern usually have a basic melody – usually (although not always) eight bars long – followed by a repeat of that same melody for another eight bars – verses 1 and 2 – followed by a different tune for

eight bars (ie the chorus) before finishing off with an eight-bar repeat of the initial melody.

You might find that you need to read the previous paragraph a couple of times before you fully understand it, but you'll find that this basic formula forms the foundation for a great many songs.

While there are many other different song structures out there, the traditional verse–verse–chorus–verse format is definitely the most popular in Western music. Here's how it's represented in music terms...

A   A   B   A

...where B is the chorus. This means exactly the same as 'verse–verse–chorus–verse', but it's certainly a lot quicker to write down.

With the basic foundations of a song in place, the next step is to come up with some chords and a melody. So, how exactly do we go about doing that?

You might already have found that some chords seem to go together, whereas some just sound wrong if played sequentially. In fact, there's a reason for this, and to understand it fully I advise you to read the chapters on chords and scales because I'll shortly be talking about the relationship between the two. If you're impatient and want to get straight on with writing your first *magnum opus*, though, hang on to your hat...

To begin with, you need to understand what's meant by the term *key* in a musical context. This is a particularly important concept to grasp, and if you're not sure what I mean when I tell you that many popular songs tend to remain in a single key for their duration, we'll be looking at that soon. Put simply, the concept of key is related to the fact that both melody and harmony are related to a single scale or tonal centre. As an example, take the C major scale:

C	D	E	F	G	A	B	C
1	2	3	4	5	6	7	1

* And certainly before this, although recording technology didn't develop to the extent that commercially based recordings were feasible until the early 20th century, and even then many early songs weren't written down, often being communicated down the generations through the unreliable method of the aural hand-me-down tradition, and are hence lost in history's blur.

If you play or hum this scale and keep the note C in the bass all the time, you'll hear how everything seems to be related to and held together by that single note:

Because of the pivotal role it plays here – it's the most important note in the scale – C is known as the *tonal centre* or *root*. So a melody derived from this scale would be described as being 'in the key of C major'. Play or hum the melody below while playing a C in the bass and you should be able to hear what I mean:

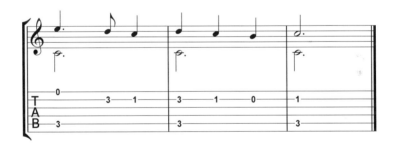

You'll probably recognise this tune as being the British national anthem, a tune widely known across the world. When you hear it over a single bass note or a single chord, what I said earlier about keys and tonal centres should begin to make some kind of sense – although if this was the only harmony we used, things would get very boring indeed. The harmony needs to move, too, and support the melody along the way, and so we need to choose some additional chords.

In order to do this, every note of the scale from which the melody is taken – C major – needs to be harmonised, and this is done by building chords on every degree of the scale. You'll recall from 'The Right Approach To Learning Chords' that C major contains three notes...

```
C   E   G
```

...and that these three notes are the first, third and fifth notes from the scale piled on top of each other:

```
C   D   E   F   G   A   B   C
1   2   3   4   5   6   7   1


        C   E   G
        1   3   5
```

So, to come up with a chord for each of the other notes in the scale, all you need to do is copy this procedure six times, beginning with the next note, D. To form a chord for C, we used the first, third and fifth notes, so let's see what happens when we use notes 2, 4 and 6:

> D   F   A
> 2   4   6

These notes played together form a D minor chord, which looks like this:

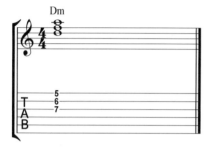

Now let's move on to the third note of the scale and apply exactly the same principle of building a chord. Here's what we end up with if we start on E:

> E   G   B
> 3   5   7

It's an E minor chord. Check it out on the fretboard:

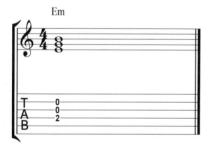

It's probably no surprise that the same maths works throughout the rest of the scale, too:

> F   A   C = F major
> G   B   D = G major
> A   C   E = A minor
> B   D   F = B diminished

So the complete list of chords that can be built on the scale of C major looks like this:

C major
D minor
E minor
F major
G major
A minor
B diminished

Play all of these chords, using the shapes I've set out below, and you should be able to hear the scale running through them. Everything seems to sound *right* somehow, doesn't it?

If you're at all unsure about how right this array of chords sounds and you can't hear how they fit the key of C major really well, try substituting one of them, like this:

Not quite such a perfect fit, is it?

I realise that this is a fairly hefty concept to take in all at once, but I'd encourage you to spend some time trying to understand it fully, as it forms the central core of everyday harmony. And I've saved the best bit for last: it works in every major key.

Here's an example to prove that last claim. First, here's the scale of E major:

> E   F♯   G♯   A   B   C♯   D♯   E
> 1   2   3   4   5   6   7   1

Now, the first thing to do is work out the first, third and fifth of the E chord, then the second, fourth and sixth of the second chord and so on, like this:

> E   G♯   B = E major
> 1   3   5

F♯ A   C♯ = F♯ minor
2   4   6

G♯ B   D♯ = G♯ minor
3   5   7

A   C♯ E = A major
4   6   1
            (8)

B   D♯ F♯ = B major
5   7   2
            (9)

C♯ E   G♯ = C♯ minor
6   1   3

D♯ F♯ A = D♯ diminished
7   2   4

And so the full list for E major looks like this:

E major
F♯ minor
G♯ minor
A major
B major
C♯ minor
D♯ diminished

Play them through and hear the scale:

Now take a look at the list we came up with for C major and see how these chords correspond to that. You should be able to see from this that, no matter which major key you're in, the 'harmonised scale' always runs the same way, like this:

1 Major
2 Minor
3 Minor
4 Major
5 Major
6 Minor
7 Diminished

Now that we have a full scale of harmonised chords, every single note of a song in one key can be backed up by a chord derived from that key's scale. Let's see what this means in terms of song accompaniment.

The first thing to understand is that nobody wants a melody where there's a chord change every note, as this might average out at between four to eight chord changes per bar – a rhythm guitarist's night in hell! Obviously, there needs to be some sort of compromise whereby one chord supports more than one melody note, if only to make our lives as accompanists that much easier.

To see how this works, let's return to the key of C major and consider one of music's very loose rules. What we want to avoid is this:

You should be able to hear that the chords here are 'right' for the melody notes but that the harmony is far too busy, rhythmically speaking; there's no flow if the harmony moves in step with the harmony. So, instead of having each note harmonised separately, the best thing to do is allow single chords to support several different melody notes. Try this:

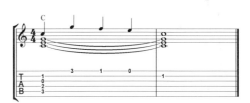

The single chord of C is quite at home with this small melody fragment over it, and if you pick apart the melody and analyse it you'll find that it centres around C and the other two notes in the chord of C major: E and G.

Now play this:

Despite the fact that we're still using notes from the C scale, it doesn't work somehow; we need a different chord. A quick look at the notes used in the melody reveals that all but one – the G – are present in the chord of F (F, A, C), so play the same melody over a chord of F major and hear what happens:

Much better, isn't it? So, the actual chords that best harmonise a melody need to contain some of the melody notes themselves in order to achieve a perfect fit. Don't worry, this doesn't put us back to square one, where we have to change chords every note; we've seen already that one chord will support a few different melody notes, as long as they're in the same general area as the chord tones. But if this is true, how many chords do we need in order to cover the whole scale? The answer is three. These three, in fact:

> C major
> F major
> G major

These chords are built upon the first, fourth and fifth notes of the C major scale, and a quick analysis reveals that they do in fact contain every note of that scale:

> C = C E G
> F = F A C
> G = G B D

If we now rearrange the notes in these three chords, look at what happens. Here are the chords:

> C E G / F A C / G B D

Put them in alphabetical order, ignoring the ones that are repeated, and this is what you get:

> C D E F G A B C

So there you have it: the whole major scale – the entire melodic range – can be covered by just three chords, which is very good news for rhythm guitarists everywhere! And,

once again, it's the same story in every other major key: the chords built upon the first, fourth and fifth notes of the scale are all you need to provide a basic harmony for a melody based on that scale. So, if you've ever heard a musician talk about a 'one–four–five' chord arrangement, this is what he or she meant.

Now let's take a closer look at these three chords. To begin with, here's the chord built on the first note of the C scale:

> C E G = C major

This particular chord sums up the key or tonal centre of any piece of music or song written in the key of C. A song written in D, meanwhile, would be summed up by a chord of D major (D, F♯, A). In music, such a chord has a name: it's known as the *tonic chord*, and it represents a sense of harmonic home.

Next in line is the chord built on the fourth note of the scale, which in the key of C is F:

> F A C = F major

Once again, this chord has a musical name, the *subdominant chord*, and it represents a sense of harmonic movement. Once the harmony has left the safe confines of the tonic chord, it usually lands on a subdominant chord and, in doing so, creates a sense of things being in transit, harmonically speaking. By this stage, the melody or song feels like it's going somewhere.

Next we have the chord built on the fifth degree of the scale – and for this one, we actually add another note:

> G B D F = G7

Take a close look at the extra note, F. If you look along the scale, you'll see that it's the next-but-one note to its predecessor, D, which means it follows the same pattern as the other notes in the chord:

> C D E F ⒢ A Ⓑ C Ⓓ E Ⓕ G A B C

At this point, it might help to refer back to 'The Right Approach To Learning Chords'.

The exact reasoning behind this promotion of the G chord to a four-note G7 variation probably deserves a chapter in itself, so I'm not going to go into it now. The short and simple explanation is that it helps the chord function in the way it's meant to – that is, as a signpost back to the tonic chord. This particular kind of chord is known as a *dominant chord*.

So, now we've mapped out three important areas of harmony usually found in a song or melody as it runs its course. The three chords most often appear in this order...

Tonic ⟶ Subdominant ⟶ Dominant ⟶ Tonic

...or, to give a music example:

‖ C / / / ‖ F / / / ‖ G7 / / / ‖ C ‖

Play the above example through a few times and see if you can hear the qualities of each of the chords. Remember that the tonic chord (C) represents home and the subdominant chord (F) movement, while the dominant is the signpost home.

Here's an example of how effective the G7 chord can be. Play through Example 1 and then follow it with Example 2, then decide which is the more effective in giving a musical signpost back to the C chord:

1   ‖ C / / / ‖ G / / / ‖ C / / / ‖ C ‖

2   ‖ C / / / ‖ G7 / / / ‖ C / / / ‖ C ‖

I'm aware that we're veering dangerously close to the subject of advanced harmony here, which isn't an area I intend to explore any more than is absolutely necessary, but I do believe that thinking of harmony in this way actually helps guitarists to understand more about chord arrangements and general song design. All good songs seem to have a natural cohesiveness about them – they just seem to *work* somehow – and the theory I've explained above will take you quite a way down the path towards fully understanding why. Songs certainly aren't made up from arbitrary series of chord changes; each has a structure, which is in fact one of its most important aspects.

So we've managed to identify three key areas of chord function. Great – but that still leaves another four chords in the harmonised scale:

~~C major~~
D minor
E minor
~~F major~~
~~G7~~
A minor
B diminished

Can we find a use for the chords built on the second, third, sixth and seventh notes of the scale, too? The answer is, yes; these chords, too, can play a part in a chord

arrangement. In order to see exactly how, we need to review how they're constructed.

With only 12 notes in the chromatic scale to choose from, it's quite understandable that we're going to find the same notes being used in different chords. After all, there are thousands of chords out there and only those 12 notes, so if two chords share a couple of chord tones, it's fairly logical that they're going to sound somewhat similar.

Take a look at this:

C major = C   E   G
A minor = A   C   E

Here we have two chords, C major and A minor, that share two common notes: C and E. Take a listen to them both in turn using these chord shapes:

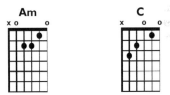

You'll probably agree that, while they're certainly not identical twins, these two chords share a strong family resemblance, and in fact we can turn this to our advantage.

We've already seen that a melody in one key can be hummed over its root note quite successfully, although harmonically this is a bit dull. We've also seen that three chords can be used to prop up an entire melody, although even this becomes a little dull after a while. So why not make use of the fact that some of the other chords in the key contain a family resemblance?

Let's go back to the UK national anthem for a moment. We could harmonise the melody like this:

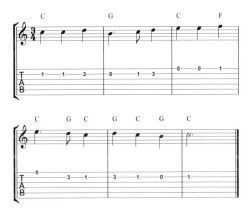

It sounds OK, but perhaps we can have something other than a C major chord sounding for all the beats in the first bar. Take a look at this:

This one sounds much better to me, and yet all I've done is take advantage of the strong similarity between the notes in the C major and A minor chords. Nonetheless, this small change has made the harmony slightly more interesting and given the tune a lift where it was needed.

There are other similarities between chords, too. Take E minor, for example.

C major = C E G
E minor = E G B

If you play both of these chords one after the other, you should be able to hear that they share a certain similarity, although arguably not as strong as that between the C and Am chords.

C E G C E   C E G C E

Despite sharing two notes in common with the C chord, Em doesn't quite fit with it; the relationship is certainly there – on paper, at least – but when you hear them both in close proximity, it's just not close enough. The main factor that prevents it from being useful as an alternative sound to C major is that it doesn't actually contain a C, so the relationship is more distant than that between, say, the chords of C and F, which have only one note in common: C. It's for this reason that the chord built on the third note of the major scale isn't used too often, as its sound is considered to be too vague. In other words, you *will* find the chord Em in songs written in the key of C, but you'll find the chord of Am far more often.

Another strong kinship between chords can be seen in the relationship between the chords of F major and D minor:

F = F A C
Dm = D F A

As you can see, the D minor chord contains an F, giving that all-important subdominant sound in C major, which makes the relationship between the two chords particularly strong. You'll often find D minor sitting in for F major in jazz standards written in C, for instance.

Compare these two chord arrangements:

1 || C / / / | F / / / | C / / ||
2 || C / / / | Dmin / / / | C / / ||

Just like the C and A minor chords, the D minor and F chords don't contain exactly the same notes, but they share enough in common to leave similar imprints on the harmony.

That leaves us with only one more chord to look at: the B diminished. In the previous chapter, I explained how the diminished isn't one of the nicest-sounding chords; in fact, its sound is so distinctive that we need to be fairly careful where we use it. Here's how it breaks down:

Bdim = B D F

Meanwhile, the only chord (apart from this one) that we haven't yet twinned with another is G7:

G7 = G B D F

So the chords of B diminished and G7 have not two but three notes in common. Surely this makes them both practically Doppelgängers of each other? Again, on paper this would seem to be so, but because the B diminished chord doesn't contain a G – the root of the G7 – the similarity is diffused:

In this case, however, there's enough of a resemblance between the diminished chord built on the seventh note of a major scale and the scale's dominant seventh for the former to understudy for the latter occasionally. This substitution doesn't happen all the time – in fact, it's relatively rare – but you will sometimes see it in jazz, particularly. Take a listen to how it sits in another chord arrangement:

<blockquote>
1 || C / / / | G7 / / / | C / / ||
2 || C / / / | Bdim / / / | C / / / ||
</blockquote>

You can hear that it's certainly having a go at signposting the harmony back towards the C chord, but the fact is that the G7 does the job so well it's very much a case of accept no substitutes!

Now you've seen how a simple melody can be harmonised by building chords on all degrees of the major scale, it's probably time to consider a few statistics. To begin with, it's all very well looking closely at the major scale and working out what goes where, in terms of chords, but what about the minor scale? Well, in actual fact, I'm not going to go into harmonising the minor scale, and that's for one very good reason: because most songs are in major keys and true minor harmony is comparatively rare. Many years ago, a musicologist by the name of Cecil Sharp surveyed hundreds of popular tunes and found that only a tiny percentage were truly minor, harmonically. He found that, even if the songs themselves were made up principally from minor chords, most of them were in fact *modal* (see the next chapter if you're not sure what this term means). So I'm by no means cutting any corners by not looking at minor harmony; it's just very unlikely that you'll ever use it, at least in the early days.

The only thing I *will* mention is that the dominant-to-tonic function still works in minor keys: dominants still signpost the home key, even if that key is minor. To see how this works, play this phrase:

<blockquote>
|| Cmin / / / | G7 / / / | Cmin / / / ||
</blockquote>

Even so, you'll notice that this progression doesn't sound quite as final as its major-key equivalent:

<blockquote>
|| Cmaj / / / | G7 / / / | Cmaj / / / ||
</blockquote>

The other thing to be aware of is the fact that, when composers write songs, they don't just use chords from a single scale; rather, part of the skill of songwriting lies in introducing interesting twists and turns to the melody of a song and making sure that, if the melody moves, so does the harmony. You're therefore very likely to come across passages of music containing chords that theoretically don't belong to the current key, and you'll certainly find songs that change key in the middle, as well as other harmonic progressions. With a little experience, you'll soon learn to treat both at face value and recognise that chords that don't belong to a key are mere visitors in a chord arrangement, while changes of key are there just to freshen up the melody or to represent a melodic change of pace. Largely, most Western songs correspond to tried-and-tested formats, and once you understand at least the basics of what's going on you'll have no trouble with them at all.

SCALES

I suppose that everyone who has ever tried to learn a musical instrument looks upon learning scales as a chore. After all, they're not really very interesting, musically speaking, and if given the choice most people would much rather spend 30 minutes or so noodling around with some songs than spending ten minutes on the scale treadmill. But what if I told you that you need to practise only a couple of scales?

There's no denying that scales are an important and often overlooked part of guitar playing, especially if you're self-taught. I used to have students come to me for lessons who were completely unfamiliar with any scales at all, and they all benefited from learning them. The fact is that scales are as fundamental to music as the alphabet is to language, as they represent the fundamental building blocks from which both melodies and chords are created. So if you're set on building yourself some technique and musical proficiency on the acoustic guitar, you'd better start in the builder's yard.

As we've seen, Western music is based on a series of 12 notes that repeat in various octaves, beginning very low and finishing very high. We've already looked at the average range of various instruments, so I won't repeat myself here, but the one fact I want you to focus on is that the 12-note scale – which is called the *chromatic scale* – is the fundamental scale from which all other scales are created.

I'm making an important distinction here by saying that this is true *in Western music*; some forms of Eastern music have an entirely different take on things and actually include intervals that are smaller than the distance between two frets. These mini-intervals are called *microtones*, and you'll probably encounter them only in blues-based music, where notes are bent slightly sharp. Of course, if you want to study traditional Japanese opera or Indian raga – two forms of music rich in microtones – that's entirely your choice; I'm assuming, however, that your musical upbringing has been Western-based and that the chromatic scale is a big enough playground for us to work in.

So let's start at the very beginning and look at all the notes of the chromatic scale in order. Here they are:

A A♯/B♭ B C C♯/D♭ D D♯/E♭ E F F♯/G♭ G G♯/A♭

Don't be concerned by all those weird-looking notes with double names, like C sharp and D flat; this is one of music's many peculiarities and doesn't affect things half as much as some people think.

The next thing to do is map out a chromatic scale on the guitar so you can assimilate it in context. Seeing as the one above begins alphabetically with A, it makes sense to start on your guitar's fifth string, which is tuned to A, and then move on to A♯/B♭ on the first fret, B on the second, C on the third and so on, until you reach the 12th fret, like this:

If you started the chromatic scale on your top E string, it would look like this...

E F F♯/G♭ G G♯/A♭ A A♯/B♭ B C C♯/D♭ D D♯/E♭ E

...and it would run up the string like this:

So each string of the guitar has its own version of the chromatic scale, between the open string down at the nut and the 12th fret. The easiest way to hear the scale is therefore to play it up a single string, like this:

I said that this is the easiest way of hearing the chromatic scale, but I expect you'll agree that it's far from being the most practical. The trick lies in being able to look past this horizontal way of approaching scales on the fingerboard and come up with something much easier to handle. In order to do that, though, we need to spend a little time looking at the guitar's vital statistics, in terms of the notes it carries.

The lowest note on a guitar tuned in the standard fashion is produced by the open bass E string. As for the highest note – well, that depends a lot on what make or model of acoustic you have. However, the average number of frets for an acoustic guitar is 20, which would make your top note a C. Whether or not it's practical for you to spend any time on the high Cs depends on the design of your guitar: if it has a cutaway, the note should fall within reach; if not, it might be a bit of an unrealistic stretch.

In any case, the lowest note on an acoustic will most likely be E and the highest around a C. But what about the notes in between? I often fox students at seminars by asking them how many notes there are on the guitar. This usually prompts some brow-furrowing while they do the maths: 'Six strings, 20 frets. That's six times 20: 120. Add in the six open-string notes and that makes 126. Right?' Nope. One of the peculiarities of stringed instruments is that there are always a couple of places where you can play the same note, and most of the notes in this equation are repeats. Pianists never really understand this concept, for some reason...

Anyway, the real solution is this. From the bass E up an octave lands us here:

Moving up another octave brings us to the same pitch as the open top E string:

The 12th fret on the top E marks the next octave:

And then we have to work our way up to the 20th fret for the top note – which, like I said, is a C. So, realistically, there are really only three octaves, plus a bit left over, which makes 45 notes. If you don't believe me, play the sequence like this and count for yourself:

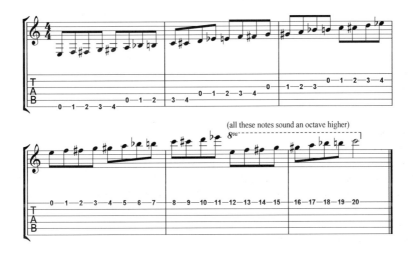

All of the other notes on the guitar are repeats, alternatives, duplicates, backups – whatever you want to call them. There are really only three-and-a-bit octaves of notes to play with, realistically speaking.

Now that that's cleared up, let's look at the dual existence enjoyed by scales and melodies on the guitar fretboard. As you probably know, you can go up in pitch either by playing up the fingerboard horizontally or across it vertically.

Horizontally:

chromatic scale
starting on A

Vertically:

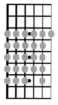

chromatic scale
starting on G

The effect in both cases is the same, resulting in the same selection of notes. The choice of which you should use at any given moment is mostly down to which is most practical and, in many cases, tasteful. In any case, these are the parameters we'll be working with while we explore the building blocks of melody on the fingerboard.

One statistic I think is worth mentioning concerns another parameter that has some control over the way you play: the reach of the hand. On a piano keyboard, a player's handspan is an important physical factor to bear in mind. There are pianists who have reputedly (and quite literally) stretched the boundaries of what's possible here. After all, if you had an octave-and-a-half span in your left hand on a keyboard, you'd probably want to exploit it to your advantage, right?

We have similar concerns with the guitar fretboard, and it's always difficult to sum up what exactly represents the average reach in terms of musical range. Certainly, if we regard the fretboard from a vertical point of view, then we should have around two and a quarter octaves under our left hands fairly easily:

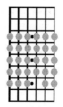

Fingers $\begin{cases} 1 \\ 2 \\ 3 \\ 4 \end{cases}$

scale of G major

This scale pattern relies on one left-hand finger looking after each fret, so the basic fingering calls for a block of four frets per scale shape at any one time. The only problem with this arrangement is that, when we try to play every note on the fretboard within those two-and-a-bit-octave parameters – in other words, the chromatic scale itself...

chromatic block
showing five-
finger range

...it calls for a span of five frets, not four! So a good reach for a guitarist's left hand would have to be around a five-fret span. In other words, you'd probably need to be comfortable with this kind of stretch to accommodate a good melodic range.

Now, if you've just looked down at your left hand and thought, 'No way!', fear not; part of the essential development that all players have to go through in the pursuit of a good level of competence on the guitar involves gaining some flexibility in the muscles of their hands. This means that, whatever your actual glove size happens to be, you're almost certain to be able to achieve a good healthy span through practice – and, of course, through tackling workouts like the one in Part 2 of this book.

So, to recap, the guitar's full range – ie its number of separate, non-duplicated notes – clocks in at a tad under four octaves, and it's possible for a guitar player to accommodate comfortably two and a bit of those in one simple scale position, so that's over half the instrument's full melodic range that can be under the hand at any given moment. This is an important fact to absorb as a lot of good playing technique stems from acquiring a rationale about fingering and hand position, and here's where it all starts.

When I was younger, I had a year of classical guitar tuition and sometimes spent entire lessons looking at the logic of a range of different left-hand fingerings for playing the same phrase. It really is that important. My teacher told me that there was usually one optimum fingering for any given musical moment and that all we had to do was find and exploit it. In order to acquire this skill, you first need to build a good overview of the fretboard; this is one of the key elements that separates a master player from an average one.

Having absorbed all of this statistical information, I expect you're asking yourself, 'Well, what next?' Actually, the next thing to do is break down the chromatic scale into its more common musical units: major and minor scales. After all, all other Western scales are just edited versions of the chromatic scale, and by far the most important and the most common of these is the major scale.

The major scale permeates every form and style of Western music, from Baroque dance suites to 1950s folk songs, bebop jazz, rock ballads and on. This is the one scale that links practically every music genre on the planet

– and if you think that I'm overstating its musical importance, I'm not; it really is a vital one to learn. I'm not necessarily talking about just doing the physical work of placing your fingers on the frets, either; this scale, above any other, is the one that has to be in your head as well as your hands.

To begin with, let's look at a single-octave shape of a simple major scale in C:

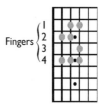

It might not be too apparent as yet, but this is in fact the scale from which most nursery rhymes are derived, and in fact most of the melodies you whistle in the shower will be derived from these seven notes, too. You can see that the way I've laid out the scale follows the one-fret-per-finger rule. However, we haven't yet covered the width of the fretboard with notes from the C scale, so in order to observe the one-and-a-bit-octaves-under-the-hand rule, we'd better extend it:

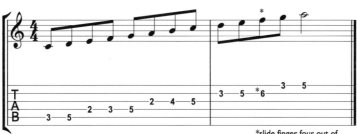

*slide finger four out of position to play this note

This is a more evolved version of the first scale, as it covers the fretboard vertically, placing the maximum number of notes within reach without the need to move the hand. Naturally, you're expected to learn this shape by heart – you virtually have to be able to play it in your sleep – and that can only be done through repeatedly playing it, every day. But before you despair, thinking that I've set you an awful lot of work, and suspecting that I'm going to insist upon you learning every shape in every key (correct, by the way!), fear not; there's a system that will make the job a whole lot easier.

If you've read 'The Right Approach To Learning Chords', you'll probably remember me mentioning the CAGED system, and if you haven't, or don't, then it's probably wise to spend a few moments browsing the basic concepts behind the system of chord construction before you carry on here. In fact, exactly the same system comes to our aid here because, just as chord shapes are built from picking out specific tones across the fretboard, scale tones are played the same way. The only real difference is that scales have seven notes in them compared to a basic major chord's three.

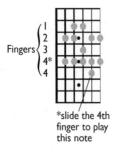

Fingers { 1 2 3 4* 4

*slide the 4th finger to play this note

It might look like nothing more than a random glob of notes plastered onto the fretboard, but look at what happens when I shade in the chord tones:

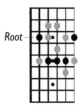

Root

You should be able to see straight away that this scale shape corresponds to the A shape from the CAGED system. By extension, it must follow that, wherever the A shape falls in any major key, you should be able to play this scale shape to match it. In other words, if the previous scale is the A shape for C then moving it up a couple of frets will give us D major:

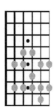

So, as with the system for learning major-chord positions, all you really have to do is learn this one shape and you've got a basic guide to how to play it in all 12 major keys. Hopefully, this makes the task of learning scales seem far less daunting than it did a few moments ago.

I wouldn't be surprised if you're ahead of me on the next

point, too: if there are only five basic major-chord positions in the CAGED system, there must be the same number of major-scale positions, too, right? Right. If you can familiarise yourself with just five basic scale shapes, you'll be able to play each in all 12 keys, which means that you'll know 60 scale shapes covering the entire fretboard.

So let's take the CAGED system for scales to its logical conclusion and explore the other four shapes available to us. First the C shape:

C shape

12 fret—

Root

Now the G shape:

G shape

8 fret—
Root

Then the E shape…

E shape

8 fret—
Root

…and, finally, the D shape:

D shape

10 fret—
Root

In each of these examples, the chord shape is outlined to help you identify each in turn and hence learn each scale shape faster.

You'll also notice that there are some places in these five scale shapes where a scale shape covers five frets rather than the more traditional four. In these cases, you'll need to stretch either your first or fourth finger out of position and reach for the note by sliding to either the left or right. This procedure can take a while to master but, as with the chromatic scale, a four-fret span isn't enough to reach all of the notes necessary in many instances, so it's a skill worth acquiring in the practice room.

Major Scales

So now, having looked at each of the major-scale shapes in turn, let's look at how exactly to go about learning them.

Firstly, forgive me for repeating myself but at this stage it's vital to remember that in learning these scales you're doing two things at once: you're gaining dexterity in and co-ordination between your right and left hands, and you're beginning to input some very significant musical information into your brain. I've already explained how thoroughly the major scale permeates modern Western music, but I'll go further to say that acquiring a thorough understanding of this one scale, both physically and aurally, will increase your powers of musicianship tenfold.

In order to play these scales with the right hand, I'd advise you to use the 'i m' fingering convention outlined on page 73 in the 'Fingerstyle Technique' chapter. If you find working this way a little tricky, using either the thumb or index finger wouldn't be the worst crime you could commit, but you should still work on that right-hand

fingerstyle technique independently with the aim of working it into your scale practice eventually.

Now here's a method for inputting this data directly into the head and fingers. To begin with, it's important to become familiar with each of the shapes individually, so spend a couple of minutes playing through each one every time you sit down to practise. When you reach the point at which you can play through each with no mistakes (and don't even think about playing them faster than two notes per second at the moment), start to treat them as a single entity and practise all five shapes in a single key. (Don't forget to change key regularly here so that you don't become more familiar with some shapes than others.) In order to do this, you'll need to refer back to the neck-chart diagram you (hopefully) drew up in the chapter on chords, as the system of alignment at work here is identical to the one involved in mapping out barre chords: just line the root of the scale up with the appropriate note on the fingerboard and play the scale from there. As this is already a task with which you might be familiar from your work with barres, it should come as second nature here. Remember, the rules are exactly the same: if you can already locate the barre versions of C, A, G, E and D, finding the respective scale shapes should be a walk in the park.

The exact method you should employ for playing through each of the five shapes is this: always begin and end on the root of the scale. This is absolutely vital so that the musical data contained here is absorbed correctly. Your ear should become familiar with the sound of a major scale and will only do so if it's presented with the notes in the correct order. So, if you want to practise the C-shape scale in E major, for instance, you should do so like this:

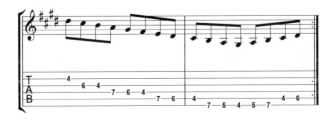

Begin with the root on the fifth string, play up to the top of the scale and return past the root to the bottom of the shape, then play back up to the root again. Have a listen to Track 3 on the accompanying CD to get an idea about how this should sound.

To recap on the learning process for the scale version of CAGED, follow these pointers:

- Familiarise yourself with each of the scale shapes separately.
- Put them in sequence order.
- Change key regularly.

You really only need to play through the CAGED scales once per day in order to keep the information fresh in your head. Don't worry about playing them too quickly, either; being slow and methodical here will get the job done. In fact, bearing in mind that part of the reason you're doing things this way is to feed the musical information into your head, the slower the better!

While you're working on the major scales, feel free to read the next section on minor scales, but I would advise against trying of the exercises in that section just yet. Instead, wait until all the major scales feel natural under your hands and until you can play them all over the neck with ease. Once you can do this virtually error-free, move on to the minors.

Minor Scales

The whole concept of major harmony in music is pretty much cut and dried. There's only one type of major scale – just one sound to get used to hearing, a few different shapes to learn and hey presto! Everyone goes home happy. Minor scales, however, aren't quite as straightforward, mainly because there isn't just one single, definitive minor scale to work with. Instead, there are three.

A major chord and its minor equivalent are different by only one note: the third note in the scale, or the middle note in the basic triad. Take a look at this:

Cmaj = C   E   G
Cm   = C   Eb G

Listen to these two examples played consecutively and you should be able to hear what I mean:

Note that in the previous example the only difference between the chords of C and C minor is that in the latter one note has been moved back one fret – it's literally been *flattened* by one degree. This is all it takes to move from major to minor – as far as chords are concerned, at least; things aren't quite that simple when it comes to scales:

```
C major = C   D   E   F   G   A   B   C
          1   2   3   4   5   6   7   1

C minor = C   D   Eb  F   G   Ab  Bb  C
          1   2  b3   4   5  b6  b7   1
```

Here, instead of just the third note of the scale being flattened, the sixth and seventh notes have been affected, too. And there's something else: remember that I said there are three minor scales? Well, here are the other two:

```
C harmonic minor = C   D   Eb  F   G   Ab  B   C
                   1   2  b3   4   5  b6   7   1

C melodic minor = C   D   Eb  F   G   A   B   C
                  1   2  b3   4   5   6   7   1
```

And here are all three of them shown together so you can hear the difference between them:

Natural minor

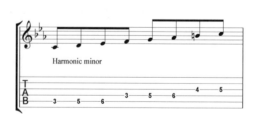

Harmonic minor

Melodic minor

Play through these scales one after another and listen hard. You should hear that the natural minor has an almost Spanish feel to it, the harmonic minor is characterised by that strange twist at the top – almost Middle Eastern in

flavour – and the melodic minor sounds only halfway there, with its flat third stuck in a major scale. In actual fact, the melodic minor has another trick up its sleeve, believe it or not, as this particular scale sounds different coming down:

This difference between the scale's ascending and descending notation – allegedly to make it easier to sing – is yet another of music's infamous anomalies. But how are we going to deal with it? Well, as you can see, the only constant factor shared by all three minor scales (at least, the only one that's not also present in the major scale) is in fact that minor third.

So how many of the scales do you need to know? If you're starting to get that uncomfortable feeling that I'm going to say, 'All three,' then relax; although ultimately it would be a good idea to familiarise both your hands and ears with the different sounds that each creates, the most common minor scale is the first one shown on the previous page, which is known as the *natural minor scale*. The other two certainly play their part in music, and you'll probably meet them all eventually, but for now let's concentrate on the natural minor.

Just as we did when we looked at the major-scale shapes, let's begin our examination of the natural minor scale by looking at a single-octave version in C:

Now, as before, I'll fill in the notes on either side of the scale so that all four frets are covered:

Does this diagram remind you of anything? This, for instance?

This particular minor scale shape for C is almost exactly the same as the C shape for E♭ major. In fact, the only difference between the two is that they start on different notes.

Now, take a few moments to absorb that information. If you thought that learning the minor scale shapes meant coming to terms with another five shapes, in fact you just need to recycle some old data. You don't need to learn a whole fleet of new shapes, just a bunch of different starting positions. And, of course, if this is so for one shape, it has to follow for the other four, too:

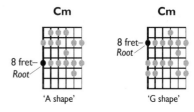

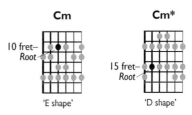

*This may be impractical on some acoustic guitars. For illustration only.

Technically speaking, this means that learning the minor shapes shouldn't take you too long; if you took my advice and spent some time practising the major CAGED scales then your fingers should already be familiar with this information and it should be just your ears that need to play catchup. So, just as before, the method for practising these shapes is as follows:

1 Familiarise yourself with the individual shapes.

2 Join the shapes together.

3 Practise them in different keys.

Once you have this system up and running – slowly and surely, with no mistakes – advance to playing all five major and minor shapes each day *from the same root*. In other words, say one day you chose to play the scales in the key of F. First of all, you'd run through all of the five CAGED major shapes in F, then you'd start again and play all of the shapes in F minor. This is an excellent workout for the ears because it means that you'll be hearing two of the most common scale forms in stark contrast, and your hands will of course be benefiting, too. The exercise makes an ideal warm-up at the beginning of a practice session.

Incidentally, I understand how this concept of one scale *shape* forming different scale *types* might strike you as a strange one at first, but in fact it's something that has been in place in music since the 13th century, so we've had over 700 years to become conditioned to this way of thinking. There's even a fancy name for these kinds of scale: they're known as *modes*. For example, A minor is a mode of the C major scale. If you want the theory proved on paper, take a look here at the similarities between the C major and A minor scales:

```
C major = C  D  E  F  G  A  B  C
          1  2  3  4  5  6  7  1

A minor = A  B  C  D  E  F  G  A
          1  2  3  4  5  6  7  1
```

You should be able to see straight away that, despite being different in every other sense, these two scales are formed from the same pool of notes. If you play them one after another, it's hard to hear a direct relationship at first, but after a while recognising such relationships becomes second nature. Every major scale has a minor running through it, known as the *relative minor* to the major key. In other words, A minor is said to be C major's relative minor. Similarly, C major is A minor's relative major.

This is a particularly neat and economical way to go about learning scales – starting from the basis that there's one basic shape and a few derivatives – because this particular trick doesn't just work with minor scales. Far from it, in fact...

Dominant Scales

So what other surprises do scales have in store for us? Well, back in the chapter titled 'The Right Approach To Learning Chords' we looked at their three basic family groups. The fun needn't stop there, however, because there's a dominant scale, too, which, like its brethren, derives from exactly the same group of notes.

First of all, let's examine the theory behind the dominant scale's construction. We've seen that the scale of C major has the scale of A minor running through it, but it also has a dominant scale – G dominant, to be precise:

```
C major = C  D  E  F  G  A  B  C
          1  2  3  4  5  6  7  1

G dominant = G  A  B  C  D  E  F  G
             1  2  3  4  5  6  7  1
```

The G dominant scale starts on the fifth note of the major scale, and so, by referring back to your diagram showing where the CAGED scale shapes occur on the fretboard, you should be able to see that the dominant starts here:

G dominant scale

8 fret–

Root

Again, it's exactly the same scale shape as C major; it's just starting in a different place. And following my system of always playing it from root to root, you'd play it like this:

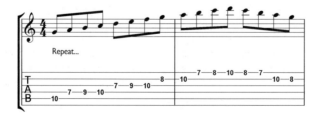

Now you should be beginning to see the benefits of learning scales with this system. You've just learned three of music's most important scale types with just one fingering, covering all the scales in all keys.

Once again, you should build upon your knowledge here slowly and methodically. Practise these new dominant scales one at a time and then begin to build them all over the fretboard. For a good scale workout, you might choose to play them all like this:

1   Pick a major key.

2   Play the CAGED major scales in that key in all five positions.

3   Play the relative minor scales.

4   Finish up with the dominant scales.

So if you picked, say, A major, you'd be playing these scale types:

A major: five positions
F♯ minor: five positions
E dominant: five positions

Not only is practising this way an excellent wakeup call for the hands and fingers but it's also absolutely priceless in terms of ear training. As your awareness of the different scale types increases and becomes more profound, your sense of music and your general ability to hear what's going on in a piece of music will increase, too.

An awful lot of guitarists' resources are concerned with understanding how songs or melodies actually work on the fretboard. Indeed, you might have spent time with a musician who, on listening to a piece, nods and says, 'Ah, I know what he's doing.' This is really how that process begins: by building yourself an aural resource like this. At present, maybe you listen to an acoustic guitar piece and think, 'I haven't a clue how he's doing that!' Well, believe me, after spending some time working through the scales listed in this chapter, your sense of musical perception will be heightened to the point at which you can at very least take a best guess about what any piece entails, scale-wise – and that has to be good news.

Other Scales In The CAGED System

At this point you might be asking, 'As there are seven notes in a major scale, and as we've found other scales that begin on a couple of the other notes, are there more scales we can find this way?' Well, yes, actually, there are. Rather than write out all of the scale shapes for each mode, however, I'll tell you a little about each one and give you a chance to hear how they sound and how to find them. Before I do, though, remember that I've already dealt with the primary scales drawn from this system; instead, to begin with I want you to concentrate on the major, minor and dominant scales. You'll encounter the others as your journey into music continues, but they'll be of very little use to you unless the foundation work has been well and truly covered.

To begin with, let's look at the modes' fancy names. You'll certainly find these words cropping up in any guitar newsgroup or forum on the internet, so it's probably a good idea to memorise them.

Taking the C major scale once again, the first scale we encounter is the major itself, whose modal name is the *Ionian* and which looks rather familiar:

Ionian = C   D   E   F   G   A   B   C

The next in line is another minor-sounding scale, this one called the *Dorian* (pronounced *door-ee-un*):

Dorian = D   E   F   G   A   B   C   D

It sounds like this:

Dorian

It probably won't mean too much to you at present, and the chances are that the Dorian mode sounds too much like the major scale for you to draw any real conclusions about it, but listen to the chord in its correct context – over a D minor or D minor-seventh chord – and things begin to make more sense.

Next in line we have the *Phrygian* mode (pronounced *fridge-ee-an*)...

Phrygian = E F G A B C D E

...which sounds like this:

It's essentially a minor scale with a flamenco air to it. Try playing it over an E minor chord to hear its full effect.

Next on from the Phrygian mode is the *Lydian* (pronounced *lid-ee-un*)...

Lydian = F G A B C D E F

...which sounds like this:

This particular series of notes forms a major scale with a dissonant twist in its tail. Play it over an F major or F major-seventh chord to bring out its subtle charms.

Eventually, you'll learn to categorise all the modes by the way they sound and be able to recognise them accordingly. As an example, I always think of the Dorian mode as being a sort of sweet minor and the Lydian as a sour major – sweet 'n' sour. (I'm big on food references.)

I've already introduced you to the sound of the C scale from G to G in the exercises above, but just for good measure this mode's fancy name is the *Mixolydian* (pronounced *mix-oh-lid-ee-un*):

Mixolydian = G A B C D E F G

You've already met the next mode, too, in the form of the natural minor scale. It sometimes works under an alias, too: the *Aeolian* (pronounced *ay-oh-lee-un*):

Aeolian = A B C D E F G A

Finally, the seventh mode of the major scale is known to its close acquaintances as the *Locrian* (pronounced *lock-ree-un*) mode:

Locrian = B C D E F G A B

Now, hang on to your hats here, because the Locrian sounds a little odd:

Even playing it over its 'home' chord of Bm7♭5 (that's B minor seventh with a flattened fifth) doesn't really cheer it up much:

Bm7♭5

So now you have a full set of scales that are all derived from the one basic series of CAGED scale shapes I showed you earlier. This means that you should now have the ability to play seven different types of scale in every major key:

7 scales × 12 major keys = 84 scales

Now, to my reckoning, having 84 different scales under your belt from learning one set of five shapes isn't a bad day's work. Your fingers will hopefully already be familiar with the basic shapes concerned; all you need to do is apply a little mental arithmetic to figure out where all the separate roots are within the scale and *voilà*! You have the full set.

Pentatonic Scales

Believe it or not, the CAGED system for scales doesn't stop there, either. There are still a couple of scales that are particularly valuable to have under your fingers, and the good news is that with these, too, you've already done most of the legwork by learning the five basic shapes.

Not all scales have seven notes like the ones we've looked at so far. In the mysterious and often just plain daft world of music, there are eight-note scales and several five-note ones, too. It's the latter type that we're going to turn our interest to now, one major and one minor, which operate under the term *pentatonic scales*. Don't worry about the fancy name for them; *pentatonic* really just means 'five-note'.

So how did these five-note scales come about? In fact, they were probably devised even earlier than their seven-note counterparts, and they're still very much in use today.

I once read somewhere that every folk culture in the world has a five-note scale of some description; Indian, Japanese and even Scottish folk music use one variation or other, and there are various theories as to why this should be so. The best that I've come across is the simple fact that they're easy to learn and simple to sing, so you don't need any musical training in order to cope with them. This is obviously an important point, if you think about the origins of true folk culture, which isn't drawn from any kind of academic resource, so these scales are representative of a sort of evolution of their own.

In any case, I expect you're dying to meet them, so here's your first, the C major pentatonic:

C major pentatonic

8 fret—
Root

Can you see the similarity between this and one of the CAGED shapes we looked at earlier? No? OK. This diagram should help:

'G shape' major

8 fret—
Root

Better? When it comes down to it, what we have here is nothing more than a pruned-down version of the ordinary major scale. Take a look:

C major scale = C D E F G A B C
            1 2 3 4 5 6 7 1

C major pentatonic = C D E G A
                 1 2 3 5 6

In other words, the pentatonic scale is missing the fourth and seventh notes of the major, but the chances are that it doesn't really sound like anything's missing when you play the scale through. After all, you've learned that the fourth tends to grate against the third in chords and that the seventh is only one fret away from the all-important root note and so would have a similar tension-inducing effect. I don't know if this is the reason why these two intervals never made it into the major pentatonic scale, but it's certainly a good enough theory to be going on with.

The point is that, even with the pruned-down version of the major scale, it's still possible to form the basic major chord.

C major = C D E F G A B C
         1 2 3 4 5 6 7 1

Becoming familiar with the major pentatonic scale shouldn't be too much of a job if your fingers already know the five basic CAGED shapes well enough; you just need to remember to leave out a couple of notes.

You probably won't be at all surprised to learn that the next scale on the agenda is the minor pentatonic, which is arguably more common than its major stablemate as it turns up practically incessantly in rock music. We'll begin with the C minor pentatonic:

Cm pentatonic

8 fret—
Root

This one should definitely look familiar, but if the family resemblance escapes you, here's a helpful hint:

'G shape' scale

8 fret—
Root

Once again, the CAGED system proves its worth and provides us with a set of pointers to remember yet another scale. Here's what the C minor pentatonic looks like:

C minor = C D E♭ F G A♭ B♭ C
          1 2 ♭3 4 5 ♭6 ♭7 1

C minor pentatonic = C E♭ F G B♭
                     1 ♭3 4 5 ♭7

You can see from this formula that the minor pentatonic is really just a pruned-down version of the minor scale, just as the major pentatonic is an abridged version of its full major counterpart. Unlike the major pentatonic, however, the minor pentatonic omits the *second* and *sixth* notes, but otherwise the essentials are there and it's still possible to make up a minor chord and even a minor seventh from the notes available:

Cm = C E♭ G
     1 ♭3 5

Cm7 = C E♭ G B♭
      1 ♭3 5 ♭7

Here are the other shapes in the minor pentatonic series. They should look almost hauntingly familiar by now:

Cm pentatonic

Major root
8 fret—
Minor root

Cm pentatonic

3 fret—
Minor root

Major root

Cm pentatonic

Minor root
11 fret—

Major root

Cm pentatonic

13 fret—
Major root

Minor root

The shapes are in fact exactly the same as their major-pentatonic counterparts but with their roots in different places – just as the ordinary major and minor scales are the same, just played from a different root note.

As you play through these scale shapes, you might find that they sound very familiar, and you'd be dead right; as I said earlier, they're used a lot in rock music. And if you're also thinking that they sound as though they're a couple of notes shy of qualifying to enter the arena of leather and sweat, you're right again.

The Blues Scale

You've probably discovered many times in life that, no matter how perfect a system you think you've found for something, there's always an exception that comes along and spoils everything. Enter the blues scale, which throws a spanner into the works of our otherwise perfectly well-formed CAGED-based machine. However, I think that, if you've come this far and you've learned the basic CAGED shapes to the extent that you can do them in your sleep, you can cope with a bit of a diversion.

The blues scale is what you might call an interesting hybrid, as it contains at least one note that doesn't actually feature in other forms of Western music at all...

The reason why the blues scale is essentially a hybrid scale is because it's really representative of two different cultures meeting head on. Anyone who has looked into the story of the blues will know that it's essentially a folk genre that evolved in the southern states of the USA, most notably in the Mississippi Delta region a couple of hundred years ago. At this time, the slave trade was rife, a shameful practice that involved the kidnapping and forced transportation of the natives of Africa's west coast to provide the US cotton industry with free labour. The blues was born out of the resulting musical clash between cultures as African timbres were grafted onto Western music forms.

Obviously, this is a very, very generalised account of the history of the blues, and if you're interested in finding out more about the blues's fascinating birth, there are whole books dedicated to the subject.

Now back to the blues scale. This quirky scale is essentially the minor pentatonic with a couple of extra nuances added to it. The first of these is this note:

Cm pentatonic

8 fret—
Root

● = ♭5

The proper musical name for this note is the *flat fifth*, although it sometimes answers to other names, including the *tritone* and even the *Devil's interval* or *Diabolus in musica*. I'm not kidding; back in the Middle Ages, this particular interval was actually banned from church music because the wise men of the day decided that it sounded so evil it was likely to summon up the Devil himself if included in a piece of music. Needless to say, the interval is a staple in blues – itself often referred to as the Devil's music – and hardcore heavy metal just wouldn't be the same without it, either!

In any case, I can assure you that you're perfectly safe if you want to include the flat fifth in your music, as years of research have proved it to be quite harmless.

Play through the following example and you should be able to hear how the flat fifth fits perfectly in the blues scale. In fact, if I write out a couple of blues licks for you, everything should fall into place nicely:

Very 'my baby done left me', I'm sure you'll agree.

The other interval missing from the minor pentatonic is the one that doesn't really occur in Western music at all. The fact is that the minor third of the scale is rarely heard at its regular pitch. We're talking about this note:

In blues this pitch is almost always played slightly sharp, which involves guitarists either bending the note slightly...

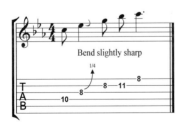

...or playing both the minor and major thirds in quick succession (a trick we probably learned from piano players, who obviously can't bend notes):

Either way around, play both the flat fifth and the slightly sharp third in a blues lick and you'll hear how things suddenly seem to fit:

It immediately makes things sound more bluesy, doesn't it?

So this is how the minor pentatonic is twisted slightly to fit in with basic blues tonality. The blues scale is in fact very adaptable, as it fits over a variety of chords in the blues vocabulary, and its influence is felt in many other diverse music forms, notably jazz.

I'm not going to investigate the individual quirks of the huge number of different music styles out there, however; all I'll be addressing here is pure music, literally the engine that powers the beast and not the icing on the cake. Just think of the blues scale as being one of the colloquialisms you'll pick up along the way as you learn the language of music.

To sum up, you should be able to see by now how the CAGED system for scales and chords is an incredible learning tool. Even if a lot of this system still seems dark and mysterious to you now, if you can get your hands around a few you'll definitely be on the correct path to follow while you go about discovering the fretboard.

More On Keys

One final thing before we leave the subject of scales for a while. I'm often asked to explain further the concept of *key* to students. It's really quite simple, but it seems to confuse many people, so if this applies to you, read on.

Many years ago, roughly at around the time of the Renaissance (c1450–c1600), music was sorted out and a mathematical template for the major scale was drawn up.

(If you're interested in the history regarding this, a quick search on the internet using the words 'equal temperament' will yield some pretty fruitful results.) Previously, semitones hadn't necessarily been equal to each other, making it virtually impossible to change key, because any new key would feature anomalies that would make any instrument sound out of tune. This problem was solved by making the semitone a standard, mathematically exact interval. The chromatic scale was thence split equally into 12 parts, each one exactly the same distance from its neighbours in terms of frequency.

So, the template for a major scale became this:

Tone ► Tone ► Semitone ► Tone ► Tone ► Tone ► Semitone

Bear in mind that a tone is two frets' distance whereas a semitone is just one fret's distance. Play this sequence up any single string and you'll play a major scale, like this one:

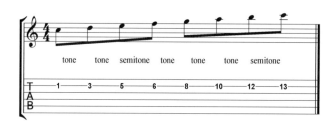

Take another look at the scale of C major to see how this theory applies to it:

```
C   D   E   F   G   A   B   C
1   2   3   4   5   6   7   1
```

The semitones fall between E and F and B and C, while all the rest of the notes are separated by tones.

This pattern applies to all other major keys, too; begin on any note and apply the same template and you'll end up with a major scale. This is why all the scale shapes in the CAGED system are the same and fully moveable, because they're little more than templates themselves.

Obviously, in order to keep those two semitone gaps in place, we need to use sharps or flats – as in the key of E major, for instance:

```
E major = E   F♯   G♯   A   B   C♯   D♯   E
          1   2    3    4   5   6    7    1
```

Here the semitone gaps are in their rightful places, between the third and fourth and between the seventh and the octave. The four sharps have been added in order to maintain the pattern, so the key of E major is said to have a *key signature* of four sharps. Each key has its own unique key signature, which is a guide to the corrections that have been made to the scale in order to keep it sounding right.*

Similarly, every major key has its own modes and chords, built on each degree of the scale. The patterns they follow are the same in each key; it's only the actual notes that change, not the relationships between them. Everything is uniform and parallel. (Refer back to 'The Right Approach To Learning Chords' if you're at all unsure about any of this.)

Playing in different keys isn't a particularly big deal for guitarists – or, at least, it shouldn't be – so we perhaps don't pay enough attention to the fact that all the keys are essentially different.

* More information on keys and key signatures can be found in any basic book on music theory. The books published by the ABRSM (Associated Board of the Royal Schools of Music) in the UK are especially good in this regard.

Practice Plan

To finish off this chapter, here's a suggested practice plan for learning scales.

1 Begin with major scales. Use the CAGED shapes to build up total fretboard coverage.

2 Change key often so that you don't get stuck in a single position.

3 Change roots and play the minor scales.

4 Play both the major and minor in each key from the same root to hear the contrast between them.

5 Map out, play and listen to the dominant scales.

6 Map out the major and minor pentatonic scales.

Once you've mastered all these various types of scales, keep them fresh in your mind by picking a key, selecting one shape and one scale type and just playing it. For instance, say to yourself, 'F major, E shape,' play it and then move on to another. Try to randomise your choice to keep you on your toes!

For further study, buy a book on scales – there are plenty out there – and audition some of music's more exotic tonal sequences. Explore things like the *diminished scale*, the *augmented scale* and the *whole-tone scale*, for example. Listen hard and decide whether or not any of them will be useful. Don't forget to come back to them every so often to re-evaluate them, too; as you progress, your ear will gradually become more tolerant to dissonance, and you might find that a scale you'd previously dismissed as unusable becomes the love of your life. Most importantly, keep an open mind about everything you hear.

OK, so those are the foundations of creating your own musical style. We all make decisions based on our own preferences, and it's through this process that we create our own unique musical voice.

FINGERSTYLE TECHNIQUE

In the world of steel-string guitar, the plectrum is often acknowledged as being king. Certainly, there are very few players of electric guitars who use their fingers rather than a thin wafer of plastic to sound the strings, and many casual acoustic strummers are to be found wielding picks, too. However, learning fingerstyle technique opens up an entire world of opportunity to the acoustic guitarist. As the man said, 'Why use a pick when you have four fingers and a thumb?'

Believe it or not, there's never really been a codified system developed for right-hand acoustic technique. In fact, I believe that over the years players have used just about every possible means to sound the strings of their instruments, and many have come up with strikingly original music as a result. Many guitarists, such as Michael Hedges and Eric Roche, have transcended basic right-hand technique and turned the acoustic guitar into a percussive instrument to help push along their highly original compositions.

Here's a list of tools with which we can sound the strings on an acoustic guitar:

- Plectrum.
- Finger picks.
- Thumb pick.
- Fingers.
- Hybrid of pick and fingers.

Quite a choice, isn't it? My own personal stance is that the best acoustic-guitar music tends to be *polyphonic*, and by this I mean that it contains different elements, such as a melody, an accompaniment and a bass line. Playing this type of music involves using more than a single plectrum; the fingers simply have to be involved somewhere, too.

Of all the above right-hand techniques, only the plectrum is associated with more *monophonic* playing (ie music that features only one of these elements). A pick is

a limited tool; even if you develop a fiery cross-picking technique, you'll never be able to achieve true polyphonic playing in quite the same way that a fingerstylist can. However, I don't want to write off the humble plectrum completely, so let's see what's involved in acquiring a good picking technique.

The Plectrum

You might be thinking that the plectrum is a comparatively new invention in the history of guitar playing, but you'd be wrong. Way back in the Baroque era, around 400 or so years ago, some lutenists would use a quill to strike the strings of their instruments. These days, of course, picks come in all shapes and sizes and are made from some surprising materials: everything from metal to stone, ivory, tortoise shell (both of the latter now banned, although you can still find old picks made from these endangered materials), nylon and plastic, for example. They can be found in a dazzling array of shapes: teardrops, kites and basically anything you can sharpen to a point – and they're all available from any good music store. So, if you think you want to learn how to play with one, the first thing you'll need to do is buy yourself a selection in order to find the one that feels right to you.

Plectrums also come in a variety of thicknesses, and this factor alone can affect what sort of sound they produce. Generally speaking, thinner plectrums (or *plectra*, if you want the correct plural) bend easily and are designed for simple chord strumming – the fact that they flex as the strings are struck somehow embellishes the sound – but they're not much good for playing individual notes, so they're pretty useless for playing scales and melodies, for example, for which you'll need a pick with a little more weight behind it. Here, a pick of roughly 1mm thickness or above generally does the trick.

I personally use 2mm plectrums for playing jazz on an archtop. If you strike a heavy-gauge string with something 2mm thick, it's going to produce a good, solid note.

Anything thinner and the 'give' in the pick gives it less impact and produces a thinner-sounding note.

Obviously, your choice of pick is very much down to your own personal preference, and most guitarists try various gauges, materials and shapes before they settle on something that suits them, but as you browse the pick selections in your local music shop, just remember one golden rule – the thinner the pick, the thinner the tone – and you should be fine.

Holding a plectrum doesn't exactly come as second nature, and it'll feel pretty weird and unwieldy to begin with, but as long as you follow a couple of simple guidelines, all should be well.

Basically, a pick is held between the forefinger and the thumb with the 'sharp end' pointing towards the guitar strings, like this:

Hold the plectrum between the thumb and first finger

Don't grip the pick too tightly or your hand will tense up, robbing you of that all-important flexibility. And in the early days you'll very probably find that you drop the pick quite often, but don't worry; this is natural when you're taking those first stumbling nursery steps and nothing to worry about. After spending some time getting used to using it and practising with it, you'll soon feel at one with this weird lump of plastic in your hand.

The next thing to learn is how to strike the strings with a plectrum. The fundamental rule here is to avoid going in too deep; using just the tip of the pick means less work for the hand. The key is to experiment. First, try strumming a chord using a pick at different depths. You'll probably find that you get the best and more easily controlled sound by using just the very tip.

As far as plectrums are concerned, there are obviously two basic strokes: up and down. A downstroke tends to carry more natural weight and will therefore emphasise a beat more efficiently than an upstroke, because naturally

with a downstroke gravity is helping your hand along whereas with an upstroke your hand is working against gravity. In general, guitarists tend to take advantage of this natural phenomenon by beginning a rhythmic song accompaniment with a downstroke, so that the first beat in the bar is nicely accented. From then on, it's pretty much a case of using alternating strokes – down, up, down, etc – although this isn't a hard-and-fast rule as there will no doubt be times when you want to include a downstroke to add emphasis and will find yourself playing two consecutive strokes of a similar type. Hopefully, by the time you start to consider refinements like these, using a pick will have become second nature.

Of course, strumming chords isn't exactly rocket science, and experimenting a little here will give you the chance to identify the parameters involved. However, take care with four- and five-string chords – D major, A major and so on – because the lower strings don't feature as notes in these and accidentally hitting them with the pick will offer up a very confused and, in some instances, unpleasant sound.

As with pretty much every other aspect of learning a musical instrument, practice conquers all, and paying some attention to your right hand when you sit down to play will drastically reduce the length of the trial-and-error period.

The next thing to look at is plucking individual strings in order to play melodies. The rules here are essentially the same as with strumming chords, but the choreography in your picking hand does need to be a little more refined. You'll still be using upstrokes and downstrokes to pick individual notes for the most part, but the pick's movements will need to be smaller and more controlled than those involved with playing chords.

A good exercise to get yourself orientated in this respect is to pick an open string using up- and downstrokes and to try to make each stroke of the pick produce a balanced note of equal volume. The movement involved with this kind of action should come primarily from your wrist and not your elbow, and you shouldn't need to tense up anywhere in order to produce a stream of nicely controlled notes. I've seen players literally hunch their shoulders and tense their whole right arm while trying this exercise, and this sort of thing must be avoided. The movement in the wrist should be no more rigorous than that needed to put out a match or shake a duster, and you should avoid unwanted tension at all costs as it can cause all sorts of medical complaints.

Now that you've spent a while trying out your picking skills on an open string, it's time to move forward and begin crossing strings. Try the simple exercise at the top of the next page:

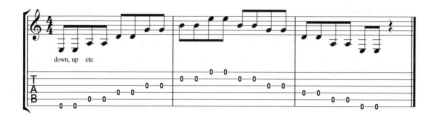

Here, all you have to do is pick each open string twice, once with a downstroke and once with an upstroke. There's a knack to playing this exercise, and you might find it infuriating to begin with, but it's well worth pursuing before you move on to anything more elaborate as it gives you the opportunity to concentrate on just your right hand without having to worry about anything you might be doing with your left.

The key words here are *evenness*, *uniformity* and *clarity*; you need to be aiming for the situation where each pick stroke produces a note of the same volume and tone, which is obviously something of an important issue when it comes to playing melodies.

Once you're sure that you're picking evenly, move on to something like this:

This is what I call a *scale fragment*. In fact, it's the first five notes of a C major scale and it serves as an ideal exercise for reintroducing the left hand and beginning to learn about synchronising both hands. You'll probably have to play it *very* slowly to begin with, as it calls for a whole new layer of control, but don't worry about that for now; your goal here should be a consistent and even tone, as the aim of this exercise is to get you to form a strong foundation to build on later. Apply all the same criteria

with this exercise as with the previous ones in this chapter and make sure everything's working before taking any further steps.

Once you're confident that everything's in place, however, you're probably best off working with scales and arpeggios to refine your picking technique further. The scales can be found in the chapter titled, rather predictably, 'Scales', while arpeggios are really naught but chords played one string at a time, like this:

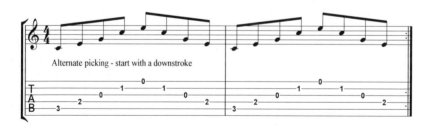

In other words, take small steps and make sure you look often at what's happening with your picking hand. I've found that small errors can start to creep in unnoticed, and these will be compounded over time and become difficult

to correct. I still give my playing technique an overhaul every so often, as I'm a great believer that you can always benefit by returning to fundamentals and reviewing everything you've learned.

Finger And Thumb Picks

Along with standard-issue plectrums, it's also possible to buy thumb and finger picks if the fancy takes you. These are slightly different to regular picks in that they're designed to be attached to the fingers and worn rather than gripped, and they look like some kind of prehistoric false nails. I'll say straight away that I'm not an expert in using them, although I have tried them out in the interests of refining my right-hand technique. For some players, though, they can be the answer to a maiden's prayer. The great acoustic guitarist Tommy Emmanuel told me that the day he discovered his idol Chet Atkins used a thumb pick was a decisive turning point in the development of his own playing style.

Using a thumb pick has the effect of reinforcing the job that the thumb does ordinarily and is really more of a consideration for fingerstylists than for simple strummers or 'plectrists'. The same can be said for finger picks, too; fingerstyle players use them to add the sort of solidity that humble flesh and fragile fingernails cannot normally give. (I'll be covering playing with fingernails later on in this chapter.)

As usual, you should experiment with finger and thumb picks, as they represent a stone it would be unwise to leave unturned in your pursuit of accomplished acoustic-guitar technique.

Fingerstyle

At this point, I feel I must raise my hand immediately and say that I think fingerstyle is the most adaptable and satisfying way of playing the acoustic guitar. It's not, perhaps, for the faint-hearted, as the job of training the fingers to play in this style takes time, but once you've done this you'll find yourself with the ability to play both melody and harmony at once.

Let me explain. Most Western music comprises a melody, an accompaniment (involving chords and maybe a bass line) and some rhythmic impetus to make it go. Playing with the fingers enables you to do all of this, whereas the plectrum caters for only one at a time. So fingerstyle is a truly polyphonic way of playing and represents acoustic guitar at its most cutting-edge and interesting.

There is, of course, a healthy precedent for this way of thinking. Take a listen to a classical guitarist playing the music of JS Bach, for instance. This kind of beautiful, polyphonic music – two- and three-part writing, with the occasional fugue thrown in for extra thrills – is possible only with fingerstyle technique and is where the acoustic guitar really begins to show its true capabilities.

First things first, though. To begin with, let's take a look at what's available to us with the fingers on the right hand.

Once again, I'll admit that there's not really any convention for right-hand fingering on the acoustic guitar; various players have their own individual ways of making things work for them – some simple, some apparently chaotic – and when they're asked about these in interviews, they usually resort to saying something along the lines of 'I just use whichever finger is handy at the time.' Not an awful lot of help!

I'm a great believer in adapting traditional methods and making them fit wherever possible, and where steel-string playing is concerned practically my total knowledge base regarding right-hand disciplines comes from a year of classical guitar lessons way back in the 1980s.

My theories in this respect are derived from the fact that classical players are trained to develop a fantastic capability with their right hands, and while the rest of us might never need to play Bach's 'Prelude, Fugue and Allegro' (BWV 998) or Albeniz's 'Asturias' at full tilt, even getting halfway there in terms of right-hand agility would probably prove to be enough in most cases.

To begin with, let's identify each of the right-hand fingers by their traditional names:

Thumb:	*p*
Index finger:	*i*
Middle finger:	*m*
Ring finger:	*a*

These four lower-case letters indicate the Spanish names for the fingers and stand for *pulgar,* meaning 'thumb'; *indice,* meaning 'index finger'; *medio,* meaning 'middle finger'; and *anular,* meaning 'ring finger'. Here they are:

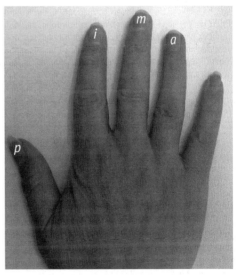

Left to right: *p* for thumb, *i* for index finger, *m* for middle finger and *a* for ring finger

Over the years, numerous players have attempted to introduce the little finger into play as well, but in many cases it turns out to be too short when the hand is in the playing position. However, you might see it in use occasionally if you choose to explore the dark alleyways of guitar music.

So, given that we have three fingers and a thumb available as grow-your-own plectrums, almost, what are we going to do with them? Well, I'm generalising here, but the thumb generally looks after the three lower strings – ie the E, A and D strings – and the top three strings are attended to by the fingers, with the index finger looking after the G string and the middle and ring fingers taking care of the B and E strings, respectively, like this:

As a general rule, the thumb looks after the bass strings and the index, middle and ring fingers look after the top three strings, respectively

Now, it's important to understand that this is far from being a hard-and-fast rule for the right hand, but it's a good place to start.

To begin with, you'll almost certainly find that your ring finger is very lazy and doesn't want to play ball, but after some patient practice it will soon develop and will prove to be at least as useful as the others. Remember that you can't rush the development of muscles, so an important watchword here is *patience*.

As with the left hand, the position of the right-hand thumb is crucial in that it has to have its own space and remain out of the way of the fingers. For this reason, guitar players tend to cross their thumb and index fingers so that they form a sort of X from the player's perspective, as shown in the picture at the top of the next column.

Note also that the wrist shouldn't appear collapsed but fairly straight in line with the forearm and with a slight hump as the hand turns in to the strings. Try to remember that there's a lot going on inside your wrist when you play,

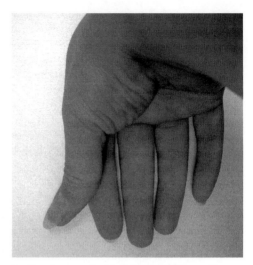

Looking down on the hand, the index finger and thumb form an X so that they don't get in each other's way

with muscles and tendons all doing their job of keeping your fingers and thumb operating, and you need to adopt a hand position that facilitates this. In other words, if you play with your wrist at a right angle to the rest of your hand, you're likely to end up in the doctor's surgery with tendonitis or worse. So don't try anything that's going to compromise free movement in your hand, wrist and arm.

In the beginning, monitor this playing position at all times. It might not feel natural to begin with, so you might find yourself flopping your wrist or introducing tension into your arm by sticking your elbow out. In a word, don't. The aim is to keep everything as relaxed as possible.

Take a look at the position of your fingers, too. Whatever you do, don't turn your hand into a claw when you play. As in the pictures above, your fingers should curve gently. As you play, you use all of the joints in your fingers, and cramping your hand up will reduce your facility in this respect. I realise that it feels odd, but just try to remember the first time you tried riding a bicycle.

Take some time to consider the exact procedure for sounding the strings, too. In the world of classical guitar, there was once a debate that raged for ages as to whether it was better to sound the string using flesh or fingernail. There were quite passionate followers of both traditions, but eventually it was decided that the fingernails gave the better sound – although there are still a few players out there who stubbornly stick to flesh. Now, this is all well and good if you're talking about the nails of the fingers and thumb coming into contact with nothing more ferocious than nylon, which is the substance used in the manufacture of modern-day classical strings. Even metallic-looking bass strings are usually wire wound on silk, so the nails don't really face too tough an opposition to their musical attack.

So a classical player takes great care of his or her fingernails, often spending a considerable amount of time filing and shaping them with emery boards before finishing them off with the finest grade silicon-carbide paper to ensure that each nail's string-striking portion (ie its underside) is as smooth and polished as possible. Articles have been written about how fingernails – and, indeed, the correct manicure – can affect tone. In other words, it's a topic that's taken very, very seriously. After all, tone is everything, right?

Players of steel-string acoustic guitars face an additional problem in that steel can do an awful lot more damage to the average fingernail than nylon, and so they have perhaps a slightly different perspective on the whole flesh-or-nails debate. For a start, Mother Nature doesn't exactly play fair, as the strength of people's fingernails varies to an alarming degree. Some people have fingernails that shred or split very easily while others have particularly weak and bendy nails and others still are lucky enough to have strong and resilient nails. The strength of one's fingernails can be attributable to diet, but a lot more, I suspect, is down to biochemistry, and to a great extent we're stuck with, quite literally, the hand that genetics has dealt us.

I'm lucky inasmuch as I seem to have acquired talons of steel on my right hand (Wolverine from the X-Men would

be proud) and so I don't run into many problems playing with nails on either nylon- or steel-string acoustics. Others, I know, aren't so lucky. So what can you do if you're one of those unfortunate people with fingernails like cheap plastic? Well, many players opt to play with the flesh of their fingers and thumb and produce some wonderful music, while many others resort to using fingerpicks and still others have to help nature along with a variety of clear nail lacquers, which can be bought at most chemists'.

A couple of players I know who tour relentlessly (and therefore subject their finger and thumbnails to quite a pounding) coat their nails with acrylic, which is available in the trendy nail bars that seem to be opening on every high street today.

This is another choice that you'll have to make – not necessarily now, but if you wanted to take your playing to a seriously high level, for instance – so I'm really just trying to make you aware of the alternatives. For now, you're best off sticking to playing with flesh, as it were, but keep an open mind and be prepared to experiment as your playing skills develop.

For the time being, sound each string with your fingertip, and be prepared to get a few blisters along the way. Who said art isn't pain?

OK, so what next? A little exercise, I think. As you'll see from the music below, for the time being I'm going to disregard what the left hand gets up in favour of focusing on the right. So it's open-string time:

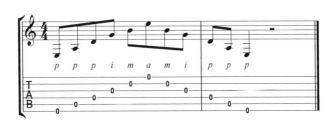

This exercise requires you to play all the open strings from low to high using the thumb and fingers. Be sure to follow exactly the fingering described here and console yourself with the knowledge that, if it feels terribly awkward at the moment, it will soon begin to feel second nature.

Next we'll vary the exercise a little and make the fingers work a little harder:

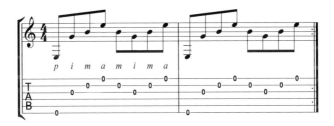

Now you're playing only one bass string with your thumb, but meanwhile the fingers are really quite busy going forward and back. Don't try reaching for speed with this exercise; it's designed to be practised over time and will help you to orientate your fingers so that they become used to plucking the strings.

The next stage is to vary the pattern we've already set up. Here, don't worry if the results don't sound too musical; they will in a little while when the left hand's added back into the frame. For the moment, though, you'd be wise to concentrate all your efforts on the right hand in isolation.

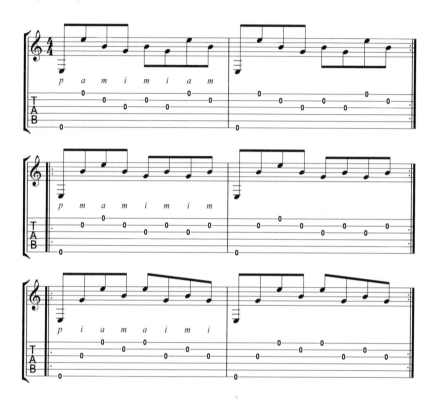

The exercises above are all designed to test and challenge your fingers and thumb. In fact, a good mini-practice routine would be to take all the exercises shown so far in this chapter and play them continuously in sequence for a few minutes. With all the twists and turns I've thrown in, after working your way through them your fingers should soon be warmed up and ready for the next step. Don't be tempted to proceed before you can do all of the exercises without making any mistakes, though, as they're designed to help you build your core technique and you

need to be sure that the foundations have been dug deep before going any further.

Now it's time to add some chord shapes in the left hand and play some *arpeggiated* chords. This term, if you're unfamiliar with it, stems from the Italian term *arpeggio*, which, as I mentioned earlier, describes a chord that's played one note at a time, in order. Arpeggios serve as a sort of halfway house between chords and scales and are very good for ear training. Your ear needs to spot the individual notes that make up each chord, after all.

The exercise at the bottom of the previous page comprises an E major chord set out as an arpeggio. Note that the thumb plays two different bass notes while the fingers do their stuff.

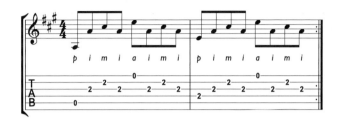

Here I've changed the E chord for one of A major and applied a slightly different choreography for the fingers. Make sure everything's working fine with this one before attempting to speed up because mistakes are always harder to put right later on.

Next try playing the simple arpeggiated accompaniment on the chord arrangement shown in the exercise below. Consider this a kind of first-level examination piece and make sure it sounds the same as the audio example on the accompanying CD before your build on it any further:

 Track 5

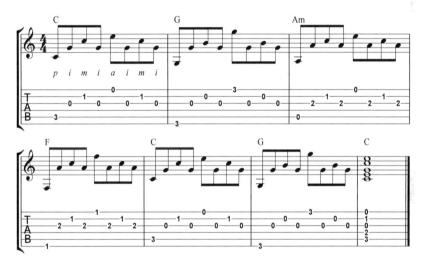

Rhythmically speaking, this kind of exercise is all very well, and quite effective for most purposes, but there are certain circumstances in which you'd want things to get a little more busy in the right hand, and this calls for some *syncopation*. This term basically means that a few offset notes are introduced to an otherwise straightforward rhythm in order to add a bit of rhythmic interest.

Now, this can be a tough concept to grasp. Pupils of mine have described the idea of syncopation as being something akin to trying to pat your head and rub your stomach at the same time (and this will give you some idea about the type of person I've been teaching), but in fact they're not far off in many respects. Take a look at this exercise:

 Track 6

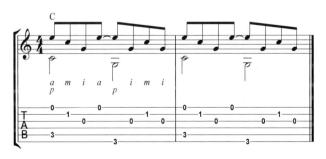

Compared to the previous exercises in this chapter, this one has a lot more going on in the accompaniment. You'll almost certainly have to tackle it at ultra-slow speeds to begin with just so you can make sure that all the moving parts are working as they should. Listen to Track 6 on the accompanying CD and try to make your version sound the same.

Playing about with offsetting the rhythm of a picking pattern can provide particularly fruitful results. The key here is to experiment and to keep a close eye and ear on what's happening in the fingerstyle world. You can learn pretty much anything from anybody, so don't be afraid to take the occasional field trip to a live music venue in the interests of doing a little research.

Realistically, that's all there is to simple fingerstyle accompaniment. True, different chords can call for different patterns, but essentially this is how everything works at the most basic level.

My advice is to try out various fingerstyle patterns on every chord you know and experiment all the time to hone your skills in this department. You'll find that some songs don't take to this kind of accompaniment, and you'll definitely need to resort to strumming occasionally or even to adopt a combination of both techniques. There aren't really any rules here; some songs benefit from really sparse backing on the guitar while others will require something more complex.

Melody

This is the other side of the performance coin. After all, you won't always be playing chords; at some point you'll hopefully be putting both chords and melody together in a neat little package. In order to pull this off, you'll need to be well versed in both melody-playing and accompaniment techniques.

The first thing to consider is that, once again, there's no official technique for playing fingerstyle melody, but in steel-string circles most players opt for the principle I mentioned earlier of using whichever finger is handy.

Another option is to use your index fingernail as a stand-in plectrum, but this can play havoc with your nails, depending on their strength and your skills as a manicurist. I use this technique occasionally, but not as much as I used to because of the heavy wear and tear it exacts on my nails. If I know ahead of time that I'll be playing a solo at some point, I'll do the conjuring trick of concealing a pick in my palm or between my fingers beforehand and using that rather than running the risk of damaging my nails.

So, in this section I'll be basing my advice on classical guitar technique, which serves as a good basis for playing melody lines. Here again we don't need to look too hard for examples; there are plenty of classical guitar works out there that feature quick-fire melodies offset against full-sounding harmonic ideas. But how is this done? Read on...

In developing a good right-hand melodic technique, you'll need to go back to doing some basic training on open strings. Look at the examples below:

This particular routine calls for the index and middle fingers of the right hand – fingers *i* and *m* – to alternate on the top string. The action required is a little like the fingers are 'walking', as they should be kept as straight as possible when sounding the string. Begin slowly and keep checking to make sure that your fingers are alternating in sequence, as any mistakes in the early days might hold you back in the future. Now try playing this one:

All I've done here is extend the 'marching' routine I set up on the top E string to all six strings. This exercise is designed to aid the basic orientation of your fingers, and I realise it will probably feel very weird the first time you attempt it. Try not to stiffen up your fingers while plucking the strings, though, as this will introduce tension and actually impair free movement rather than enhance it. Try to strike a balance between having just enough *push* in your fingers to sound the string correctly and having too much. Again, experimentation is the key here. The movement required for this exercise is actually a lot more gentle than you might suspect, and most of the movement should come from the large joint in the middle of each right-hand finger, as shown in the picture on the right.

With this exercise, too, nature helps us along a little. Take a look at your index finger when it plucks the string. All the movement is actually only 'one way' and the finger automatically springs back to the starting position each time. This is no doubt due to the cunning interplay of muscles and tendons in the hand, but from a practical standpoint it means we don't have to keep repositioning the finger after each note has been produced – a small advantage, perhaps, but certainly a valuable one!

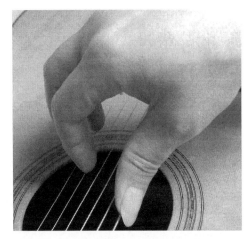

When playing fingerstyle, a lot of the actual movement comes from the large joint in the middle of the finger

This next exercise calls for both hands to be brought into play. It's a little scale fragment over two strings, similar to the plectrum exercise shown earlier in the chapter, and is designed to get your fingers used to doing some real co-operative action.

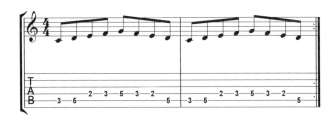

For this exercise, I want you to use two different fingerings: one beginning on the *i* finger and the other on the *m*. If you were thinking that there can't be too much difference between the two, you might be in for a surprise. Obviously, you'll need to be ready to use either finger to begin a melody sequence, so it's a good idea to start learning alternate patterns right away.

Once you find that you can play the above scale fragment smoothly and with no mistakes, begin to introduce larger scales, such as those found in the 'Scales' chapter, but be sure to take things very slowly at first. You'll get a chance to flex those fingers thoroughly in the workout in Part 2, but it might be a good idea to let them do a little more groundwork before they apply to join the fingerstyle Marines.

Playing In Time

As an aside from the topic of basic fingerstyle technique, I want to take a few moments to talk about the value of using a metronome when you practise. Now, everyone is born with a natural sense of rhythm. Have you ever watched a young child dance to music? Even at a very young age, the idea of moving one's body to music seems already embedded to a degree. It's only when we get older and the inhibitions that come with so-called maturity are cemented in place that we tend to forget this innate talent.

The same is true of pitch. It seems that most people have some sort of facility for recognising pitch and singing, whistling or humming in tune, although as with movement some fine tuning is always necessary. To develop a good sense of pitch, you'll first need to do some ear training (see the 'Ear Training' chapter for this), and to develop a sense of rhythm you'll need something to keep your own rhythm in check as you practise.

Enter the metronome. These invaluable devices are available in many shapes and sizes, the traditional variety looking like a small wooden pyramid with an arm on the front that swings to and fro, with an audible click each time, at a speed that can be set by the user. They're designed to mark out a steady rhythm as you practise.

Other designs of metronome range from smaller versions of the type described above to electronic devices no bigger than a credit card that emit an electronic bleep instead of a click. If you're really not keen on another trip to the music store, I'm sure that you'll be able to download a computer program from the internet that will play the role of patient timekeeper as you practise. Whatever type you choose to use, I strongly urge you to acquire a metronome (you're going to need one in the workout section) and *make sure that you work with it*. Doing so will improve your sense of timing no end.

When I first introduce my students to the concept of playing along with a metronome, most of them are convinced that it's going to be an easy task, and they're generally shocked to find that, on their first attempts, their timing is way out. This is actually a good thing, because it highlights another deficiency that's easily corrected.

In order to work on the exercises we've already looked at for playing melody with the fingers, you need to set your metronome to a slowish time – say, around 80 beats per minute – and pluck the string on every click, like this:

Track 6

Gradually, over time, you should be able to increase the speed setting to around 144bpm (beats per minute), but don't expect to be able to do this anytime soon; this type of training takes time and is best done in regular, short, controlled bursts rather than sudden leaps. Just be patient with yourself and things will work out fine.

Eventually, all the work you've done will pay off and you'll find yourself with a very sharply tuned sense of timing, which is essential if you're aiming to play in a band or with another guitarist.

Back To The Fingerstyle Plot

After a while, you'll need to make use of the other resources available on the right hand and introduce the ring finger, or the *a* finger. This particular digit is traditionally weaker than the *i* or *m* fingers and has the added disadvantage of being biologically tied to the little finger, too. (I'm no anatomist, but this connection has something to do with the tendons that control the fingers' movement. The thumb and first two fingers have their own independent control systems, but the ring and little fingers have to share.) Before you start asking questions about how nature could have overlooked such an obvious disadvantage, though, just remember that playing guitar was never really part of the plan when the body's blueprints were originally being drawn up.

In other words, you might find that the ring finger feels decidedly lazy when it's called upon to take part in any fingerstyle activity. Fear not, however; it can be trained up with some more patient practice, so let's get down to taking a look at some fingering conventions that employ the ring finger.

So far, we've seen that fingers *i* and *m* play melody by literally taking turns on the strings. Now we're going to have three fingers playing, so that rule has to change. We'll go back to using open strings for this:

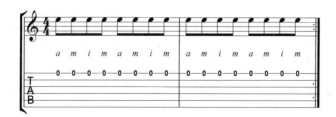

This is the kind of exercise a classical-guitar student is taught in order to introduce his or her *a* finger to co-operative melody playing. It's another exercise that's best taken dead slow, because it's going to feel incredibly tricky to begin with.

After coming to terms with this particular fingering sequence, alternate it like this:

Remember that all you're doing here is introducing the ring finger to the concept of playing melody. You won't be using either of these sequences rigidly when you play.

When I first encountered this technique, I admit that I couldn't do it at all. Subsequent arduous practice sessions convinced me that it was absolutely impossible, despite my very patient teacher telling – and showing – me otherwise. Then, to my absolute dumbfounded surprise, one day I just did it, straight through, from beginning to end, with no warm-ups and no failed attempts. I just dived straight in – and I've been able to do it ever since. To my mind, this serves as further proof (if further proof was needed) that practice works, even if it does so very slowly.

Recently I had this theory proved to me again when I wrote a piece of music that had the most infernally awkward fingering. I was seriously struggling with it at first, but I managed to convince myself that it had to be possible because I wasn't actually asking my hand to do something physically impossible, and then, hey presto! It worked. I think much of the work required to cope with this kind of problem is based in mind over matter, so take your time with this one and try it every day for a couple of minutes at a time. After a while probably something will just click and you'll be able to play it.

Needless to say, once your ring finger has been trained to jump through hoops, a whole world of possibilities concerning the melodic capability of the right hand will be opened up to you. The best way of completing this training regime is very similar to the way we've been working elsewhere: begin with single-string exercises before advancing to scale fragments over two strings and then on to complete scales. Take it slowly and gradually increase your metronome speed over time until you're comfortable with around 120bpm.

(Incidentally, if you're interested in training up your left and right hands even further, you'll probably find a classical tutor by Mauro Giuliani titled *Studies For Guitar* useful. This book focuses entirely on exercises for the right and left hands and is an old friend from my days as a classical student.)

Another resource that we have available to us, melodically speaking, is the thumb. This particular digit isn't overlooked by orthodox classical technique, either, although in the classical pieces I've played its role is quite often limited to fingering a melody on the lower strings. Anatomically, of course, this makes sense, given the rigours of classical-guitar fingering, although steel-string players use it more adventurously. The fact is that the thumb offers quite a wide surface area to be applied to the string and can help produce some nice, full, fruity notes. Jazz guitarist Wes Montgomery used his thumb almost exclusively for playing melodies during his career as a guitarist and produced some startling results, reaching a very impressive turn of speed and demonstrating exactly how versatile this seemingly clunky digit can be.

In other words, I'm ruling nothing out. I'm not going to insist that you adopt the classical style of fingering exclusively; all I'm saying is that it's a very good place to begin disciplining your hands. The rest is up to you.

Dynamics

Now it's time to spend a little while considering exactly how the right hand influences the dynamic range of your playing. Here the term *dynamic range* applies to more than mere volume increases, encompassing instead the overall flow of any piece or accompaniment figure. You don't need me to tell you that an acoustic guitar doesn't come with a volume control* and so the only real influence you have over the volume of your playing is the way you use your hands and sound the strings. However, bear in mind that each instrument will have a different dynamic range, too, so it's a good idea to take a few minutes to explore here exactly what kind of control parameters are available to you.

In all my years of teaching, one thing common to all acoustic-guitar students is that they play too quietly, almost

---

* Unless, of course, it's an electro-acoustic model and you're playing through an amplifier or PA system. I thought I'd better mention this before I get floods of email!

as if they're afraid that their instrument will explode if they put any force into what they're doing. I realise that modern domestic arrangements mean that playing at any kind of volume in the average family home is often considered an unsociable act of an almost diabolical nature, but even so you should refer to the chapter on 'Establishing An Effective Practice Routine' to pick up a few pointers on dealing with this kind of situation.

So, given that this part of your training is going to be a little noisy, find yourself somewhere tucked away from the rest of the family – or suggest they all go to the cinema without you – and get ready to test the dynamic range of your guitar.

It's fairly obvious what's necessary here: you need to know how quietly you can play and also how loud. However, there's another very important factor to take into consideration, too. Playing the guitar is all about tone; guitarists go to extraordinary lengths to make sure that everything they play sounds, well, *nice*, aiming to find that sweet spot where their instrument gives its best and then basing their playing around it.

As you're exploring how quietly you can play, you'll need to bear in mind that, if played below a certain volume, every guitar begins to sound thin and reedy. Also, putting too much energy into the strings can cause them to sound out of tune, thanks to a scientific phenomenon I really can't explain to you here, having opted out of science at school as soon as I possibly could. Basically, the strings over-vibrate and begin to sound sharp, so you'll need to find this level and make sure you stay well clear of it when playing.

Perhaps now you can see that, when I'm talking about an instrument's dynamic range, I'm referring to the range that's useful to us when performing. In fact, locating this usable range is a fairly easy thing to do; all you need is, as I said earlier, a bit of peace and quiet. Start with a few chords, playing them very quietly at first and getting gradually louder. There'll come a point beyond which you lose the reediness and produce a nice tone that should then serve as your benchmark for quiet playing.

The other end of the scale is easy to find, too. Play a few chords, making sure that you put as much energy into the strings as you can. You'll soon find the point beyond which things begin to sound harsh and unmusical, and this point is effectively the top end of your dynamic range. Then, imagine you're turning your hi-fi's volume control up and down and practise playing from very quiet to very loud a few times so that the parameters become set in your mind. I was once told that a good acoustic guitar sounds at its best when it's giving out around 85 per cent of its available dynamic range.

Dynamics play an integral part of pretty much every form of music. It's the ebb and flow between loud and quiet that makes a piece work. If everything was played at exactly the same volume, it would soon become boring, no matter how inventive its melody or harmony.

Tone Control

Having established that your acoustic guitar didn't come with a volume control, you've probably discovered by now that it didn't come with any tone controls, either. Even the tone controls on an electro-acoustic are designed to adjust just the overall tonal spectrum of the instrument for either recording or performing purposes and don't really take into account the type of subtle tone adjustments that are necessary during a piece.

So what can you do to control the tone of your playing? Actually, quite a lot, especially if you've chosen to play with your fingers rather than with a pick.

To begin with, it's time to take a few more tips from our classical-guitar-playing cousins. When a classical player wants to play a particularly bright sound on his instrument, he'll pluck the strings near the bridge, so try doing the same. Gently strum a chord around the soundhole of your acoustic and then repeat the same chord but this time strum it closer to the bridge. You should hear a difference comparable to that produced by turning up the treble control on an amplifier: things become much brighter and sound slightly more metallic.

Meanwhile, playing only a centimetre or so away from the bridge will give the resulting sound a sort of percussive thud. This feature can be useful as a special effect, but in most cases you'll need to avoid it by playing a little further away from the bridge. Even so, make a mental note about how far away from the bridge the best-sounding brightness lies and try playing there if you ever want to give a bit of texture to what you're playing, such as song accompaniments.

Now try playing at the other end of the tonal spectrum, near the end of the guitar's fretboard. This is where the sweeter, more subtle tones are located. Some players even play over the fretboard itself in order to accentuate this effect. Indeed, it's good to be aware of what kind of tonal variations exist in your instrument simply by experimenting. Just play around with your guitar – and take a look at what other players do with theirs, too. You might not have seen those subtle changes of position before, but now you know why they're there!

Hybrid Right-hand Technique

The only other right-hand technique in popular use today is a hybrid technique that employs the use of both pick and fingers. With this technique, an ordinary plectrum is gripped between finger and thumb in the conventional manner, but the remaining two fingers – the *m* and the *a* – are used to provide arpeggiated accompaniment and melody. The advantage of using this technique is, obviously, that it gives you the best of both worlds: you have the full use of the pick when necessary, if you're playing single lines, but you can then use your fingers when things begin to get busy or syncopated. Meanwhile, the bass notes are generally more pronounced in the same way as they are when using a thumb pick.

To be honest, this technique is most often used by electric-guitar players – particularly country players, for some reason – but I thought I'd mention it here to give you another option to consider as you consolidate your right-hand technique.

As far as actual exercises are concerned, I'd recommend that you try arpeggiating a few chords while using this technique to see if you think you might want to develop it. It's never been one that I'd wholeheartedly recommend to anyone who's just starting out, though, because it ties up two perfectly good, usable fingers. However, this is really just my personal opinion. In fact, hybrid picking is a technique that works for a few very good players and whatever I think certainly shouldn't put you off exploring it for yourself.

String Damping And Muting

One thing that's particularly difficult to control on the acoustic guitar is the exact length of chords and individual notes. Once a note is plucked or struck with the pick, it will keep on ringing until either you remove your finger from the fretboard or the string vibrations stop naturally. If a chord contains open strings, though, you can't just lift your fingers from the fretboard to stop the strings from ringing; instead, you need to find a way of damping or muting the strings so that everything you play remains clear and pronounced. The established way of doing this is to use the fleshy edge of the right-hand palm to touch the strings lightly to silence them, and this trick takes a while to learn.

Have a go at this simple test and you'll soon see what I mean. Take a look at this E major chord:

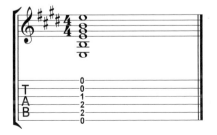

Play the chord quite loud, let it ring for a couple of seconds and then remove the fingers of your left hand from the fretboard. The chances are that the A, D and G strings will have quietened down nicely but the bass E and treble B and E strings are still going about their business without a care in the world.

Now bring the edge of your right hand down to rest gently on the strings just in front of the guitar's bridge. Everything should go deathly quiet. This is right-hand muting in action.

Beginners often complain that their rhythm playing sounds untidy because the individual chords they play aren't sufficiently defined and everything sounds a bit of a mess. This problem usually stems from the fact that they haven't yet learned to mute efficiently. Needless to say, it's another thing that's often omitted from the practice routine, so it never really has much of a chance to develop.

Muting is a simple enough technique to start working with. All you need to do to develop it is play a few chords every day, letting them ring on and then cutting them off using your right hand, listening closely to what's going on. Experiment using different pressures, too, and try incorporating the technique into your rhythm playing. Many folk stylists from the 1960s and '70s used to slap the strings to mute them and used the percussive thump that this action produced as part of a song's rhythmic drive.

Left-hand Muting

The other side of the coin is muting with the left-hand fingers. You've already seen from the E chord experiment described above that lifting the fingers from the strings tends to quieten them – although sometimes it causes the open strings to sound, which can cause problems in itself.

The trick behind left-hand muting is to lift the fingers gently, just enough to damp the string and stop it vibrating, rather than remove them completely

For the sake of symmetry, try a similar experiment here by placing a barre across all six strings and play them. Now lift the fingers of the left hand from the strings completely and listen. You've probably successfully stopped the barre from sounding, but you might have created a mush of open-string noises in its place. Try the same thing again, but this time release the pressure from the left-hand finger yet leave it in place and listen again. The strings should stop vibrating completely and the result should be silence.

By practising how to apply different variations in pressure with the left hand, you should find the point at which you can produce the correct effect with only a very slight hand movement.

Left-hand muting is a technique that's used in conjunction with right-hand muting to control the general sustain situation with chords or melodies, and over time you'll begin to be able to judge when to apply it.

There's one other muting technique you need to know, and it too concerns the left hand. I suppose it should be called the 'whichever finger is spare' muting technique, because there are times when you need to mute open or unwanted string-ringing with the left hand instead of with the right. You might be in the midst of a fairly busy rhythmic passage and literally not have the option of using the right hand to mute. Here, you'll quite often find that you have a left-hand finger going spare to lay across the strings to mute them.

This isn't an easy technique to describe, so here's a picture showing my left hand finger lying across the strings to silence them as the other fingers hold a chord position:

In this picture, my index finger is holding down a note and my third finger is muting the lower strings

It's another technique that will feel cumbersome and awkward at first, but all of my students pick it up quite quickly out of a need to silence those ringing strings!

That just about all you need to know about fingerstyle technique for now, although I encourage you to watch other acoustic players in live situations and position yourself somewhere where you can see exactly what's going on with both of their hands, as this will give you a chance to pick up some valuable pointers. There are players out there who have perfected some rhythm techniques whereby they use the body of the guitar like a drum to produce percussive effects, for instance, although this type of thing really goes beyond the scope of this book. Luckily, these days there are resources like the internet and live DVDs that will enable you to explore the technique further and help you make your own discoveries.

LEFT-HAND TECHNIQUE

We've already looked at general playing position, and you've hopefully come to understand how important it is to position your left-hand thumb correctly when fretting either chords or scales on the fretboard. (If not, refer back to 'The Right Approach To Learning Chords'.) There are a few other things to be aware of here, however.

As far as possible, you should aim to play with your fingertips rather than with the soft pad of your finger, as your fingers will tend to hit other strings and mute them if allowed to 'lie down' on the fingerboard. Of course, when you're dealing with stretches and the fingering requirements of certain chords, you'll find that it's not always possible to play with the tips of your fingers, but it's a good general rule to do so wherever possible. Take a look at this picture:

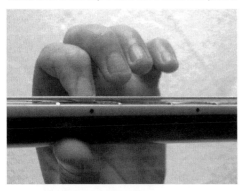

You should aim to play with the tips of your fingers rather than the fleshy pad

Your fingers should be positioned at the back of the frets as far as possible, too, as this will produce the cleanest note, as shown in the picture at the top of the next column. Again, however, this isn't always possible because some chords actually call for other left-hand fingers to get in the

way, but it's always something to aim for, so use your judgement. If any muted or buzzy notes show up in chords, however, put finger position at the top of your checklist while you sort it out.

Try to position your fingers close to the frets to get good, clean notes

Spare Fingers

Naturally, in many situations when you're playing chords or melodic passages, you'll be putting only one or two left-hand fingers on the fretboard at once, leaving you with a couple of spares. And I have some advice to pass on here, too...

I've seen players lift their fingers from the fretboard and virtually stick them up in the air if they're not using them, and this is a very bad habit. Spare fingers should hover above the strings and not be positioned otherwise, or you'll end up with all sorts of unwanted tension in the hand. Think of it in terms of playing a single note on your guitar.

What feels more comfortable? This...

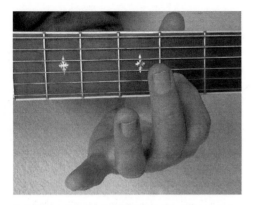

One finger plays a note while the others flap around in the air – a waste of energy!

...or this?

Here, the fingers that aren't in use on the fingerboard are held as close to it as possible, thus saving energy

In the first example, I've lifted my fingers clear of the fretboard and kept them there, which is a waste of energy, whereas in the second I've merely relaxed them and left them hovering over the fretboard, totally free of tension.

It might sound like I'm nitpicking here, but honestly it's these kinds of things that can affect your fluency on the instrument and can spell the difference between a melody passage or chord change being hard or easy to play. Just remember that, with a relaxed hand, you shouldn't need to make any extra movements.

Vibrato

Vibrato is an Italian musical term that refers to a slight variation in pitch that's applied to a note after it's been plucked, bowed or sung. You've probably heard a kind of shimmering effect that seems to pack in some kind of added emotional information to a melody note, typified by the oscillation of a long note played on a violin or the warbling

of an opera singer. That's vibrato in action, and there's no doubt that it's the single most important technique for an acoustic-guitar player to master. Listen to a range of different players and you'll hear that their vibrato characteristics all vary slightly in the same way that they all have different yet highly individual handwriting. It can affect an individual's style and sound enormously.

It would be tempting to believe that vibrato is a technique that applies primarily to electric guitar, and it's certainly true to say that vibrato is far more exaggerated in electric blues or rock guitar than acoustic guitar, but the fact is that even classical guitarists have to learn how to use it, so it's definitely a skill worth learning.

Basically, there are two different types of vibrato available to acoustic-guitar players: classical vibrato and rock/blues vibrato. The main difference between these two is the manner in which the finger manipulates the string with each. With classical vibrato, the finger moves along the string, whereas with the rock option it moves it from side to side.

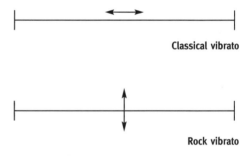

Classical vibrato

Rock vibrato

This means that the classical style of vibrato is more subtle in that it doesn't cause the string to move as much as the rock style, resulting in less of a deviation in pitch.

Let's look at classical vibrato first. Here, once a note is struck, the finger moves forward and back along the length of the string slightly in a gentle rocking motion to produce a very slight waver in the note's pitch. (I've demonstrated both types of vibrato on Track 8 of the accompanying CD to give you a good idea about the sonic differences between the two.) This movement should start in the wrist rather than the fingers and is very similar to that of gently shaking something with your left hand. I've even heard one player describing it as being like trying to hold onto a plate of wobbling jelly! It takes a lot of practice, but if you apply the rules you've already learned in this section to isolate the technique and practise it for a couple of minutes a day, you should find that things soon start to improve.

Rock vibrato, meanwhile – which, as I said earlier, is most commonly associated with light-gauge strings and electric guitars – involves moving the string from side to side with the finger. Rock guitarists often add quite a lot of vibrato to the notes they play by just increasing the side-to-side movement of their fingers on the string – something that's comparatively easy with a set of .009-gauge strings but slightly more tricky on an acoustic guitar set up with fairly heavy strings. You need pistons for fingers to achieve the same sort of pitch variation on an acoustic, in fact, which is why few of us even bother to try.

On acoustic guitar, rock vibrato is most commonly used to shape a note – ie to add some of that shimmer I mentioned – and nearly always gives a melodic passage a kind of bluesy ambience.

Meanwhile, the physical side of rock or blues vibrato is slightly different to its classical counterpart in that it requires you to push and pull the string sideways rather than merely roll your finger along its length. It's harder

work, in other words, but it's a technique that's still well worth mastering.

I usually teach the 'slow motion' technique for achieving effective rock or blues vibrato. First of all, I give my students a slo-mo demonstration of how vibrato is added to a note so that they can see exactly what kind of movement is involved. I then encourage them to try the same at dead-slow speeds and allow them to speed things up only when the basic machinery is running properly. Obviously, I can't show you how this works in a book, but I'll describe the sort of action you'll need to perform.

To begin with, play a note on one of the unwound top strings – either the top E or B – and then push the string slightly 'up' towards the other side of the neck. Then let the string's natural tendency to straighten itself take over at the top of the push and then pull it 'down' towards the lower edge of the fingerboard. Here's a couple of pictures showing the upper and lower reaches of the vibrato:

 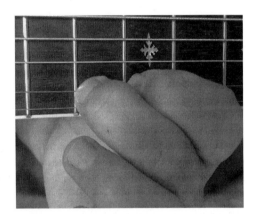

Here's the extreme end of the vibrato spectrum – not quite as far as many people think!

Here I'm not moving the string too far in either direction; just enough to give that shimmering effect to the note. Listen to Track 8 on the accompanying CD for more information and for a demonstration of the slow-motion principle in action.

Vibrato is yet another technique on the guitar that calls for a lot of patient practice – I don't think I've ever taught a student who has picked it up straight away – so don't be discouraged if things don't appear to be working immediately. Time and patient practice will improve things, and you'll soon be adding vibrato without even having to think about it.

Again, you should listen to different acoustic players to find out what sort of vibrato they add to their melodic lines. This will provide a quicker and more effective guide to when best to apply it than anything I can tell you!

String Bending

As with vibrato, string bending is a technique that's most commonly associated with the wilder side of rock and blues playing and makes the fullest use of lighter gauge strings. The acoustic guitar, meanwhile, has a disadvantage in this regard in that its third string – the G – is wound, whereas on an electric it's a plain string and hence easier to bend. Because of this, and because of its heavy-gauge strings, string bending on an acoustic is usually kept to a minimum in everything except acoustic blues playing, and even then it's not half as wild as string bending in electric blues.

The basic technique of string bending involves pushing or pulling a string up in pitch, usually towards the next note in the scale. If you want to experiment with this particular technique, try this: place your fingers on the guitar's B string, as shown here:

Apply pressure with your index and middle fingers behind your ring finger to give your string bending a little more push

Now sound the note one fret up from the third finger – this is the one you're bending the pitch of the note towards – then try pushing the string with your third finger until it reaches the target pitch.

Difficult, isn't it? Try to leave the other two fingers in place on the string and make sure that your thumb applies an opposing force against the push. It doesn't matter if your thumb decides to hook itself around the back of the neck; in fact, this will help give your finger something to push against.

As I say, bending isn't a technique used by many acoustic players, and few of its exponents use it as much as electric guitarists, in any case, but it can still add an effective, bluesy edge to your playing and so is worth investigating.

Sliding

Sliding is the practice of moving a note up or down in pitch by merely sounding the string and sliding your finger along it, either up the fretboard or down it, to produce what's classically termed a *glissando* (which means 'swoop', incidentally). You might not think that there's much to learn here, but if you experiment with the technique, you're sure to discover two things:

1 It hurts your finger.

2 It's harder than it looks!

I normally find that students need their brakes checked when they first try to slide, as it's really a question of knowing

where and when to stop. When practising this technique, as with string bending, you need to set yourself a 'target pitch' (although here, of course, this needs to be a lot higher than the note next door) and then try sliding from one note to your selected target pitch, awarding yourself points for accuracy and grace. It's important that you don't rush here or your playing will begin to sound nasty, and you should always make sure that what you play sounds good.

Hammers And Pulls

These two techniques might sound like they belong to an Olympic sport, but what's in a name? In actual fact, the art of hammering or pulling a note is concerned with sounding the strings with the left-hand fingers rather than with the more standard right-hand pick or pluck.

In order to explain the technique, try this experiment. First, place your first left-hand finger on the fifth fret of your guitar's G string, but leave the third fingering hovering, like this:

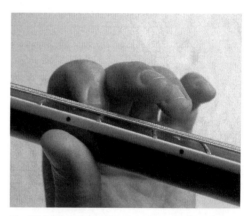

The third finger is ready to hammer onto the string

Sound the note by plucking the string conventionally with your right hand and then immediately afterwards bring your third finger down on the string with medium force. The result should be that you've just sounded two notes from one right-hand pluck. If you in fact achieved only one and a half notes, you'll need to repeat the procedure until you're able to produce two notes of equal volume with a single pluck. The only difference between the two notes should be in their actual dynamics: the plucked note should have an abrupt picked sound whereas the hammered note should sound smoother. The difference will be subtle but you should be able to detect it.

A pull – sometimes known as a 'pull-off' – is the reverse of a hammer. To play such a beast, you need to pluck the note under your third finger and lift it to sound the note under your first, as shown here:

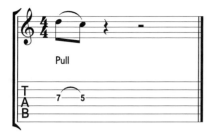

The chances are that, this time around, you'll find that the first note sounds clearly but the act of removing the third finger from the string has the effect of muting the second note. This problem is quite common and can be remedied by very slightly dragging the third finger as you remove it from the string so that you're virtually plucking the note again. This isn't always necessary – in faster scale passages, for example, sometimes the speed of the notes and the energy in the string combine to give you a clear pulled note – but sometimes it helps.

That just about covers the major techniques carried out by the left hand, and by paying attention to all of them individually during your practice routine you're sure to be able to bring them on line. Just remember that practically everything on the acoustic guitar can be achieved by the three Ps: patient, persistent practice.

ESTABLISHING AN EFFECTIVE PRACTICE ROUTINE

It might surprise you that most of the time guitarists spend practising is completely wasted. After years of teaching at seminars and so on, I've come to the conclusion that a typical practice routine runs something like this: play through everything you know and put the guitar down after about half an hour, telling yourself that you've had a good, worthwhile session. I can't tell you how wrong this approach is. Fortunately, it's quite easy to put right.

One of the most common factors that holds guitar students back is an ineffective or totally disorganised practice routine. We're all guilty of it; we settle down on the sofa in front of the TV and sit there, strumming the odd song or playing a couple of licks we've played 100 times before and calling it 'practising'. Wrong.

In the same way that walking upstairs a couple of times is no substitute for going to the gym – although arguably it *is* exercising – and resisting the last doughnut in the box isn't exactly dieting, playing stuff that you already know isn't practising. Instead, you need to be playing material you *don't* know in order to make any noticeable advances. This is the only way to really power forward, as it means you're constantly challenging yourself. A good teacher will be aware of this and will make sure that there's enough new material in your practice routine to ensure progress. The practice routines of self-taught guitarists often omit this vital element, however, and they often end up in the Doldrums. I've had so many students arrive on my doorstep with very much the same story – 'I'm in a rut and I don't seem to be making progress any more' – and nearly always their problem has been caused by a loss of direction in the practice department.

Of course, the workout in Part 2 is designed to put you on the straight and narrow path of true practising, but there are some other factors that will definitely help you along the way, too. To begin with, it's helpful if you can turn your practice time into a daily habit, in the same way that people who are into fitness have regular times when they either go out jogging or down to a gym. It's much the same with

guitar playing: we need to develop stamina and build muscles, too, but thankfully, perhaps, only in a comparatively small area of the body.

So let's consider what needs to happen before you can build the perfect practice routine that will guarantee progress. To begin with, you need to look at your environment.

Your Practice Space

I'm well aware of the constrictions that modern-day living imposes on guitarists; indeed, it's partly why I wrote the original *10 Minute Guitar Workout*. At that time, I had countless pupils who led busy lives with demanding, often stressful jobs, partners, children and all the other issues that come as part of being alive today. One thing they all had in common was the fact that even making space to practise was a huge problem. True, it's quite rare to find a home with enough space to have a whole room dedicated to playing guitar, and yet it's important to have somewhere to go that's quiet and away from all unnecessary distractions.

The worst of these distractions is the TV. As I mentioned above, many would-be guitarists try to practise while sitting in front of the TV, and this leads to two things: poor concentration and bad posture. So what's the point? I need you to promise me one thing: that if you're at all serious about improving your guitar playing, you'll find 30 minutes or so each day that you can dedicate entirely to playing your guitar. If you're really pushed, keep up the ten-minute workout from Part 2, as this will ensure that your technical facility continues to develop. However, in order to input any new material, you're going to need the additional 20 minutes.

Tuning

So, assuming you've found somewhere quiet to practice, what's next on the list? Well, the first thing you should do every time you pick up the guitar is check its tuning. I recommend that you use an electronic tuner here as it will guarantee you the accuracy that your ears might not yet be able to provide. Ears, like muscles, take time to develop (refer back to the 'Ear Training' chapter to see what I mean here), and you need to discipline yourself on this point because practising on an out-of-tune instrument just isn't worth the effort. Keeping the guitar at a constant pitch is very good for the ears as they develop, too, so make tuning your first job of each practice session.

Warm-ups

Next, you'll need to warm up. Playing through the charts you'll find later in the book will serve you well here, as they're designed to function partly as warm-up exercises. If you don't want to play these, however, or if you're having a rest from the guitar gym, take a couple of minutes to do some gentle stretching exercises – slow scales are quite effective here – or indeed anything that will limber up both hands.

Don't mistake this section of your practice routine for a time to build stamina, though. Don't worry, I'll be addressing this area later on, but you wouldn't expect an athlete to run a 1,000m race from cold; they stretch and prime themselves gradually to ensure that they're at the optimum level of readiness when the starting pistol fires. There's a good reason for this, too: 'cold' muscles won't perform as well as those that have been warming up for a while beforehand.

Scales

The next part of your practice time should be devoted to building stamina and developing muscle, and scales are ideal for this – as are arpeggios, if you fancy a change. You'll need a metronome to practise these effectively, though.

I used to give my students scale fragments to play against the clock, gradually increasing the speed on the metronome when I was sure that they'd reached an appropriate level of fluency. We even made a game of it; once they were familiar with the CAGED system (see 'The Right Approach To Learning Chords' if you're unsure what this is or how it works) I'd say something like, 'A major, C shape,' and they'd do the mental arithmetic to work out where the C shape for A is on the fretboard and play it at the speed at which the metronome was set. This enabled me to keep an eye on how they were getting on with learning the fretboard as well as how their aptitude with either pick or fingers was coming along. I'd give them two or three different scales to play in this way before moving on. (There's no need to spend too long on one single element of a routine if time is limited, and I certainly didn't want lesson time to become a relentless slog for them, either.) I'd make a note of how fast they were playing the scales comfortably and suggest how far they should go in order to push for the next setting on the metronome. In

making it a challenge like this, I made sure it remained fun, yet all the time they were developing their technical co-ordination and forming the bedrock of their general playing technique.

I encourage you to follow the same path and make a note of how you progress in terms of speed. Literally make notes like this...

Feb 9
120bpm

...so you can monitor your rate of progress. Doing this requires you to play the dual role of teacher and student, so be very strict with yourself and don't try to play too quickly until your chosen scale is completely error-free at the level at which you're currently working.

Works In Progress

Now it's time to address all of the issues raised so far in this chapter, and here I'm going to hop onto my soapbox for a few moments.

I've seen so many pupils play me something, make a mistake in the middle and say, 'I always get that bit wrong,' and they're usually quite surprised when I reply, 'OK, but have you ever tried to do anything about it?' For some reason, students are quite happy to let mistakes creep into their playing but seldom take steps to put any of them right. Again, this is a bad practice habit you should always try to avoid. Problems like repetitive errors can become easily embedded in a piece of music, and if they're not dealt with, they'll stay there forever. I've proved this to myself many, many times; whenever I decide to spend a nostalgic few minutes playing through some classical pieces that I was learning over 20 years ago, you can bet that *all the mistakes are in exactly the same places as they were back then*. They obviously weren't completely dealt with at the time, and they certainly haven't cured themselves over the years, despite the fact that I'm definitely a better player now than I was back then.

The truth is that problems with playing are like bumps in the road: they won't fix themselves; somebody has to come along and deal with them. With a little training, though, that person could be you.

Today, I teach everyone how to act as their own 'doctor' so that they can diagnose exactly what's going wrong and put it right. So let's go to guitar medical school...

Musical First Aid

I'll warn you in advance that you might need to read this section a couple of times before it begins to make sense. To begin with, though, I believe that the ability to recognise and deal with the problems that occur in your playing is one of the most valuable resources you can learn.

In my experience, all problems that guitar students encounter with their playing usually fall into one of two categories: *musical* and *technical*. When I hold seminars, I often ask the students to name me as many common problems with playing as they can think of, preferably from their own experience. I then write these two words on a blackboard as headers and we start to categorise each problem as it comes up. We might come up with things like, 'Left- and right-hand co-ordination is poor,' which we file under 'technical', and 'Not being able to play what you hear,' which is filed under 'musical', and so on. After a little while, the list ends up looking something like this:

TECHNICAL	MUSICAL
Left and right hand co-ordination	*Not being able to play what you hear*
Fluency with scale passages	*Not knowing which key you're in*
Trouble with changing chords	*Problems with working out recorded solos*
Inability to get a good tone	*Difficulties with improvisation*

I generally find that, at around this time, the students are beginning to get the point: that problems which stem from the more technical side of playing are actually distinctly different from those of a purely musical nature. In other words, the technical side of the blackboard gets filled up with problems relating to the actual physical interface between player and instrument – simply learning to operate the machine efficiently – while musical problems mostly relate to learning the language of music itself.

This difference between musical and technical problems is similar to that between hardware and software in the world of computers: hardware is concerned with machinery while software encapsulates the programs designed to run on that machinery. These two sides of computing spring from two very different but interlinked, compatible industries – manufacture and programming, essentially – and so thinking of the problems in this way makes it easier to see that we should address each type with a different set of strategies.

Once the differences between musical and technical problems are made clear in this manner, you can set about solving them by making changes to how and what you practise. I've found, for instance, that physical problems

can usually be solved with good old-fashioned repetitious practice and that musical problems almost exclusively need to be addressed with some specific ear training.

Have a go at drawing up your own list of problem areas and categorising them as being either musical or technical in nature. Just getting used to dividing problems up in this way will go a long way towards solving them.

In order to help you see what sort of remedies I'd recommend for the list above, I'll deal with them each individually just as I would if I was conducting a seminar or a private lesson.

Technical Problems
Left- And Right-hand Co-ordination

If this was a one-on-one session or a group class, I'd get you to show me a specific phrase or area where this problem always shows up. In other words, I'd want to see what happens so I could give you some idea of how to fix it. If it occurred during scale practice, the first thing I'd have you do is slow everything right down – I call this 'imposing a speed limit' – because it's quite likely that you've tried to speed things up too soon, in which case the whole process will need to be reviewed. This speed limit would be in place for a couple of weeks, during which time I'd encourage you to look very carefully at what both of your hands were doing in terms of picking, finger action, how they were positioned, etc, and make sure that everything is working smoothly at a slow speed. This would usually be enough to highlight any problems quite quickly.

I once had a student who had exactly this problem – he could play fluently up to a point against the metronome and no further but couldn't work out why – and I applied exactly this strategy to solve it, getting him to slow down and taking a long look at what both of his hands were doing. Although he promised me that he was sure his picking was strictly alternate, I noticed that when he reached his 'speed limit' his picking began to fluctuate and he had a tendency to introduce random pick strokes, which seriously impaired his fluency. He was completely unaware of this, but once I'd pointed it out to him and told him to go back a few notches on the metronome for a couple of weeks so he could concentrate on fixing the problem, he was soon able to regain his original speed and in fact exceeded it shortly afterwards.

Fluency With Scale Passages

Problems here usually have similar origins to co-ordination problems in that they nearly always stem from some kind of malfunction in one hand or the other. Again, the best thing to do here is impose a speed limit and take a good long look at what's going on at slower speeds, which is usually enough to pinpoint the glitch and repair it. Sometimes, however, the solution isn't always that simple.

I once had a student who had exactly this kind of problem, with symptoms very similar to the student whose co-ordination problems I described in the previous section, in that his playing began to fall apart after a certain metronome mark had been reached. In his case, however, his left- and right-hand co-ordination was spot-on. At first I couldn't see what was going wrong, but I did notice that his left hand began trailing a little and tensing up as if it was having to work too hard, so I asked to examine the student's plectrum and found that it was possibly a bit on the large size. I swapped it for one of my own and that solved the problem instantly. So sometimes it's necessary to look, look harder and then look even harder and think laterally before you can spot what's causing a problem.

Changing Chords

Problems with this aspect of playing are usually very specific in that they generally occur at one point in a piece the student is learning. Every would-be guitarist has problems with changing chords in the initial stages of learning because they're asking their hands to do some new and unfamiliar tasks and so will have to expect the occasional revolt.

Similarly, if you're having trouble with a tricky chord change, it's quite likely that you just haven't come across that particular change before. You might find yourself thrown back to the drawing board because your hand hasn't been in that situation before and needs to learn the necessary movement.

The solution is to take the chord change out of the piece completely and make it part of a mini-practice plan. I liken this to having the song up on the workbench, taking it apart and fixing one piece of it before you can reassemble it and carry on. Don't play the song again until you've practised the change on its own for a week or so's practice sessions. Once you've done this, you should be able to play through the song without stumbling at the problem area.

Sometimes it's a good idea to maintain a record book containing all these kinds of glitches and run through each of them every time you practise. Taking the problem area out of a piece and dealing with it in isolation should defuse it effectively.

Getting A Good Tone

Problems with tone are fairly common and can usually be solved with another complete overhaul of playing technique. I usually advise my students to review even the most basic elements of their technique at regular intervals, getting

them to make sure that their picking or plucking is still on track, for instance, and that their hands and fingers are in the optimum positions. Where poor tone is a problem, it's nearly always *not* the guitar's fault, and yet it's always the first place players look to isolate the cause of the problem. However, when I pick up the student's guitar and play it for a few minutes myself, it invariably sounds fine (and after spending many years reviewing instruments for guitar magazines, I can usually spot a duff instrument from a mile away). Then, of course, I find myself confronted by comments like, 'Oh, it sounds OK when *you* play it,' as if the whole problem's suddenly my fault.

Half the time, it's a case of the player not putting enough energy into the string, and this is certainly true of acoustic players. After all, even the best acoustic guitar is going to sound thin and reedy when played at a certain level, so I often recommend that they try playing angrily for a few moments, literally to take out their frustration on the guitar. Quite often, this makes all the difference.

However, there was another case that foxed me for a while. One evening, a student I'd been teaching for a while came in with his usual guitar and I noticed as soon as he started playing that it sounded unaccountably dull and lifeless, so I took it from him and played it myself, but nothing I did brought it back to life. So I began to look for signs of physical change on the instrument itself and noticed that the strings above the nut seemed a bit wet. I remembered that he'd previously had problems with strings sticking in the nut, which had made tuning the instrument very awkward for him, and to remedy this I'd recommended that he apply the tiniest amount of either lip balm or Vaseline to the string grooves. When I asked him if he'd done what I'd suggested, he replied, 'I didn't have any lip balm or Vaseline, so I used washing-up liquid. I thought it would do the same thing.' After a string-change and a clean-up, his guitar's tone returned to normal.

Musical Problems

So much for the technical problems. Now it's time to take a look at some problems that are more musical in nature.

Not Being Able To Play What You Hear

Many people hear music in their heads (don't worry, this isn't the same as hearing voices) – the perfect guitar solo, for example, or a fabulous melody line or great harmony part – but when they pick up their guitar, the solo, melody or harmony has gone, or at least is somehow out of reach.

The ability to transfer music from the brain to the hands can be developed with ear training, but it takes time. There's a whole chapter in this book devoted to this aspect of musicianship (titled, unsurprisingly, 'Ear Training'), but here's a brief glimpse at what has to happen.

I believe that music is a form of non-verbal language and that learning to play an instrument involves becoming familiar with the ins and outs of that language. It's simply not enough to learn to play songs parrot-fashion if you want to play at a level beyond beginner to intermediate.

It's a little like the difference between learning enough French or Spanish to get by while you're on holiday and learning enough to actually live in France or Spain and hold a decent conversation. Unfortunately, many guitar students stop at the former level without realising that achieving the latter doesn't take much more time. Instead, they're nervously content to remain tourists and never get to experience the joy of being able to parley with the locals.

When I start teaching a new pupil, the chances are that they've never been exposed to any of music's inner workings – scales, arpeggios, etc – and so their ears aren't tuned in to what's happening within a piece of music. In fact, these days I can predict pretty accurately which area students need to work on when I find out what style of music they've been playing. For instance, rock players might have spent time learning the minor pentatonic scale all over the fretboard, attuning their ears to its sound in the process. However, the minor pentatonic is only five notes out of a possible 12, so their ears have trouble with any music that draws from the rest of this vocabulary.

So the problem of not being able to play what you hear is nearly always solved with some ear-training exercises like the ones outlined earlier in this book. As your grasp of the language of music grows, you'll be able to hear more of what's going on in every piece you hear.

Not Knowing Which Key You're In

This is actually a more specific version of the previous problem. You should be able to obtain a sense of identifying keys by systematically practising scales and playing – and humming or singing – exercises like this one:

By hearing every note from the major scale in relation to its root, you should get a grasp of the concept of key fairly quickly as the dominance of the scale's root is repeatedly emphasised.

Working Out Recorded Solos

This is yet another extension of the basic principles outlined above, except that here the music is coming from an outside source rather than inside your own head.

Another adage that I think is very true in music is, 'If you can hum it, you should be able to play it.' In this regard, you'd be surprised by how many people can't hum what they're trying to play, let alone play it, so I teach players how to identify notes, hum them and then find them on the fretboard. It starts as a game: I play a note on my guitar (with the pupil not looking, obviously) and then they sing it. It's a process of trial and error at first, but many of them are surprised by how quickly they start to be able to find notes that they can hold in their heads. By humming the note, they're turning something from outside their heads

into something that's very much on the inside. By literally inviting the music in, the job becomes much easier.

The next part of the job is really just an extension of the first. There's a lot of software out there that will slow down music from CDs and MP3s while maintaining the correct pitch, making it really easy to work out solos or melody lines. (I use one called Transcribe!, available from www.seventhstring.com.) If you've schooled yourself in the basic skills of listening, humming and playing, you'll find yourself managing the task faster and faster.

Improvisation

This is a huge subject and so it's not surprising that many people encounter problems associated with it. By far the most common problem is with creating solos and song ideas that all sound the same, and it stems from working with an incomplete vocabulary.

In order to play and improvise well, you really need to know the language of music inside out, just as you'd need to know a lot of French vocabulary if you wanted to hold an actual conversation with a native French-speaker. You simply can't get by with a phrasebook-style relationship with music; if you really want to make progress, you need to achieve a degree of fluency in the language of music.

Here's a simple test: can you hum a chromatic scale? It sounds like it should be simple enough, but it comes as a real shock to many music students when they become hopelessly lost.

Here's the chromatic scale in standard notation:

The chromatic scale spells out the musical alphabet, and if you can't recite it then your ear hasn't been trained enough to be able to carry out manoeuvres like transcribing – and much of the music thrown at it won't make sense, either.

Another valuable skill is being able to transcribe chord arrangements from a recording. In fact, this is usually a combination of two separate skills: the ability to hum and then find the root of a chord. The best way of doing this is first to work out if the chord is fundamentally major or minor and then take it from there.

The next step is to play lots of chords and arpeggios and learn how to hum them. With my students, first I play them a chord and then they try to hum the notes it contains. While this sounds pretty difficult, again I usually find that people surprise themselves by being able to break down a chord in this way after only a short while. Once you're familiar with the basic mechanics of major and minor chord types, humming one type is actually very similar to humming the other.

The underlying point here is that, if no one leads you towards doing this type of exercise, you probably won't end up going there voluntarily, telling yourself it's too advanced. And yet we teach our children the alphabet at nursery!

Hopefully you'll see from the problems I've identified here how necessary it is to become a DIY music doctor if you want to advance in music without the aid of a teacher, and also how vital it is to challenge yourself continually in order to maintain the cutting edge of your playing.

It really is a good idea to devote part of your practice routine to ensuring that both the musical and technical sides of your playing are healthy and, if not, to develop

the resources necessary to spot a problem and then deal with it.

Fun

The final part of your practice routine should be devoted to having fun. This is the time to play through the songs you've learned and just let yourself go. This will give you the chance to maintain your repertoire and make sure that everything you've learned is still in good working order.

How Long?

That just leaves one more frequently asked question to deal with: how long should a practice routine last? Well, my *10 Minute Guitar Workout* book proved to thousands of people that ten minutes of organised practice each day is enough to keep a technical edge, but obviously it doesn't leave any room for learning new material. If, however, you can spare 30 minutes a day on top of doing the workout exercises shown in Part 2 of this book, you'll definitely see some progress – as long as your practising remains functional and doesn't drift off into directionless noodling.

However long you've set aside for practice, though, remember to leave time for each of the sections I've outlined in this section:

- **Tuning**
- **Warm-ups**
- **Scales**
- **Works In Progress**
- **Fun**

After tuning up, for instance, you could safely divide your time between the other four sections proportionately, which in a 30-minute practice session would mean that you'd spend around two minutes tuning and seven minutes on each of the other sections. Of course, these are mere guidelines; learning the guitar doesn't have to be as disciplined and precise as a military campaign. I can assure you, however, that if you pay attention to the tasks I've outlined here, you'll be making some very good progress, very soon.

PUTTING IT ALL TOGETHER

I've already shown you how scales represent the builder's yard from which melody springs, and how chords go together to form an accompanying harmony. Surely it's now just a question of putting the two together? Well, in a way, yes...but, equally, no. (I know, I know – I'm beginning to sound like a TV science correspondent.)

I usually recommend to students that they start working on songs or pieces as soon as possible, firstly because it's motivating to hear something forming from out of all the hard work and secondly because it's important for them to be able to hear the skills they're learning in context. I'm quite open about what they learn and generally I leave the choice of style completely up to them, because music is music, after all, and you'll find very similar things occurring everywhere, in terms of the actual mechanics involved. The only time I ever step in and offer advice is if I think the choice of material is too advanced, as this can only ever lead to frustration and dashed hopes. The perfect balance is something that's challenging but not out of reach. At this point, many of my students go out in search of songbooks of one kind or another in the hope of learning some songs, and you won't be surprised to find that I have some advice here, too:

- Be prepared for the chords in the songbook you choose to be completely and hopelessly wrong.

- The arrangement transcribed in the songbook won't necessarily be taken from the same version of the piece that you have in your CD collection.

Now, it's true to say that things have improved vastly since I started teaching full-time, back in the 1980s. In those days, music publishing still didn't really know what to make of modern rock or pop music, and so the music books published at around this time tended to reflect this, in that they often missed the mark entirely – so much so, in fact, that I would spend a fair amount of lesson time writing out the correct chords for students and advising them to refer to their books as nothing more than a guide or, in desperate circumstances, a lyric sheet. (Imagine a hopeful, eager student arriving on my doorstep with a book of AC/DC songs transcribed for piano and you might begin to see what I was up against!) Back in those days, the job of transcribing music from pop and rock albums was given to music students, who were told not to make anything too complex. Many of these students weren't guitarists (hence the prevalence of piano notation) and so many of the chords were best guesses.

Things reached crisis point at around the mid-1980s, when something must have clicked somewhere and it became almost mandatory for guitar music to be presented in both standard notation and tablature. Accuracy suddenly improved by a factor of ten, too, and manuscripts claiming to be note-for-note representations of the original recordings started to spring up everywhere. I still often found rock classics notated in the wrong keys, impossible-to-play chord symbols and other gaffes, but in general songbooks published around this time are much more accurate.

Today, magazine newsstands sag under the weight of numerous guitar titles, books and tutors, while CD-ROMs, DVDs, the internet and a host of other learning tools serve to raise awareness about exactly what a student of the guitar needs to cover in order to become proficient on the instrument. Despite this, however, it's still probably a good idea for me to cover here exactly what you can expect when you land yourself some printed material to play on your guitar.

Songbooks

These are still by far the most common resource available today. The principle should be straightforward: you like the songs on a particular CD and so you seek out the music book, go back home and play it. Easy, huh? Well, almost. There are still a few things that could trip you up, so we'd better spend a few moments considering them.

To begin with, you might find that the music in different songbooks is laid out in drastically different ways. For instance, you might find books that contain just lyrics and chords, like this:

C   F   C

Old McDonald had a farm

In my opinion, this type of book should be avoided, as it gives you virtually no information. Actually, I think these books are on the decline now, mainly thanks to the availability of more accurate and useful books for approximately the same cost. (Incidentally, beware of any book that claims that it's possible to play all of the songs inside with just three chords. It usually isn't.)

Next up are the books that contain melodies, lyrics and chord names, like this:

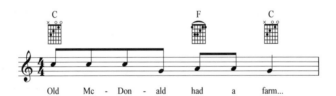

These books are generally meant to be available to as many instrumentalists as possible, hence the lack of tablature and very general chord symbols. They obviously offer no clue as to the actual accompaniment required, leaving you to do the hard work in determining exactly what fits the mood of the song, or even winkling out what was played on the original. It's a detective story, although the basics *are* there. Most of the jazz 'real books' are written out this way, for instance.*

Now here's a variation on this type of book:

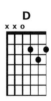

We still have the melody, lyrics and chord names from the previous example, but this time there are little chord boxes over the top of the music, too, that serve as an *aide-memoire* for those students having problems with remembering chords.

This is all well and good, of course, but sometimes the chord symbols aren't right – or, at least, they're not the same as those in the recorded version. Music publishers are still wary about putting anything in a book that appears too hard, and so these books often contain lowest-common-denominator chord symbols over the top of the melody. These simplified chords certainly don't render the music useless, but you do have to be quick-witted enough to know that if you see this...

...the artist on the original recording might actually have been playing this:

* They're called real books because a long time ago, collections of popular songs were sold under the counter and called 'fake books' because, in theory, all a musician needed was the melody and chords of a song in order to be able to fake a performance. They were illegal because no copyright was paid to the composers, hence the cloak-and-dagger sales technique. Eventually, major publishing houses took over, paid the composers and produced real books instead.

It's the same chord, but it's not *exactly* the same, if you see what I mean, and the difference can make...well, all the difference.

Arguably the most common type of songbook layout these days is the standard-notation-plus tablature variety, which looks something like this:

In this example, the guitar part has been transcribed from the original recording note for note, and so little, if anything, is left for you to do other than learn it and play it. The only thing to watch out for is left- and right-hand fingering and fretboard positions. Quite a lot then, really!

The fact is that a transcriber will nearly always be working to a CD performance of the song, with no visual clue as to what the guitarist is up to (DVD performances are still a luxury in this context), and as it's possible to play the same notes in different places on the guitar, it's easy to see that the transcriber's art involves an awful lot of educated guesswork. I often transcribe music for magazines, and when I do I try to present the most playable version I can muster and yet one that resembles the original as closely as possible. But that doesn't mean I always get it spot on...

Also, some players are renowned for having their favourite fingerings for chords or highly personalised ways of playing melody lines, and unless the transcriber is aware of this, it's possible that the fingerings they produce might not correspond. This discrepancy used to crop up in lessons so often that I gave it a nickname: the quirk factor. I'd write out a perfectly playable version of a tune for one of my students and then I'd see a video of the guitarist who originally played it performing it differently, sometimes with very awkward fingering. Every player has individual habits, of course, idiosyncrasies that they've acquired at some point during the learning process and which they see no reason to correct as long as they work, and this can make things darned difficult for the transcriber.

I'm nitpicking here, of course, but be prepared to find incorrect transcriptions in songbooks, usually after you've spent hours learning them. So keep your wits about you and don't take any published transcription of a piece as holy script; it's only by maintaining a healthy cynicism that the strongest survive!

Finding Your Way Around

So, once you've bought a book of songs or pieces, you should be set up for an easy time of learning some music, right? Well, in theory, yes, but you might have to learn a little Italian along the way, too. We'll be attending Italian For Musicians classes a little later in this chapter, but for now let's look at the navigation skills you'll need to acquire before you can find your way though a piece of written music.

To begin with, it's usually much easier to find your way through a transcription if the material you're learning is a song, because the lyrics will serve as a guide and you'll be able to match them with the music to find out where you are. Keeping track of where the verses and choruses begin and end is a great way of establishing markers as you explore a piece of music.

I generally encourage each of my students to listen to the original piece while they follow it in the book, too, which is another easy way of getting them familiar with the written version.

Keep a pencil handy, too, so you can mark the page at strategic points if there's something that you specifically want to learn. It's possible that you won't want to learn the whole piece but instead cherrypick its key moments – great chord changes or nice melodic moments, for example – and earmark them for later inclusion into your own ideas.

Counting

If the piece you're working on is an instrumental, with no lyrics to guide you, the task of listening to the original while reading the score becomes slightly more involved. A good trick here is to count through the piece by taking note of its time signature and tapping your pencil on the page as you count off the bars. So, if you came across a section that looks like this...

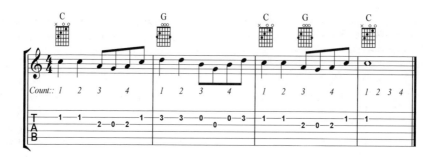

...you'd no doubt notice that the time signature – the two numbers stacked above each other on the left-hand side of the stave, resembling a fraction – is 4/4, indicating that that there are four beats to each bar. You'd therefore need to count it like this:

‖ 1 2 3 4 | 1 2 3 4 | 1 2 3 4 | 1 2 3 4 | 1 2 3 4 ‖

This time signature, known as *four four* and sometimes indicated by a **C** symbol, is by far the most common (hence its other name: *common time*) and you'll certainly come across it often as you peruse written music. Other time signatures that crop up often are 3/4 (usually thought of as *waltz time*) and 2/4, which is generally used in military-sounding music, such as marches.

The system with these two time signatures is the same as that for 4/4. You'd count a 3/4 tune like this...

‖ 1 2 3 | 1 2 3 | 1 2 3 | 1 2 3 ‖

...and a 2/4 piece like this:

‖ 1 2 | 1 2 | 1 2 | 1 2 ‖

Of course, you'll be aware by now that the world of music isn't at all rational, and this is true of time signatures, too. Sometimes you'll see time signatures that don't have the number four as a lower digit; instead, these will most likely bear an eight instead. These time signatures are dealt with differently, so it's worth spending a little while familiarising yourself with them. You might come across 6/8, for instance:

If you're thinking that this must mean that there are six beats to each bar then you're very nearly right. In fact, the pulse of each bar is grouped into two groups of three, like this:

‖ 1 2 3 – 1 2 3 | 1 2 3 – 1 2 3 | 1 2 3 – 1 2 3 | 1 2 3 – 1 2 3 ‖

Counting a piece as I've described here can obviously become quite confusing after a while, especially if the tempo is fairly fast, so you're best off counting a 6/8 piece like this:

‖ 1 2 3 – 2 2 3 | 1 2 3 – 2 2 3 | 1 2 3 – 2 2 3 | 1 2 3 – 2 2 3 ‖

Eventually, you'll begin to feel that there are two main beats to the bar, at which point you'll be able to count just the pulse, like this:

‖ 1 2 | 1 2 | 1 2 | 1 2 ‖

I don't have the space here to cover all of music's many time signatures, but the examples I've listed here are by far the most common. If you want to explore this area further, you'll be glad to know that there are plenty of books available that cover the theory of time signatures.

First Steps

OK, so we've established that it's a good idea to look through the music with an accompanying recorded version in order to help you map out what falls where in very general terms. What next?

Without doubt, a very common syndrome that you should definitely take steps to avoid is trying to do too much too soon. It's never a good idea to try to play through a whole piece straight away, as you'll most probably soon be overwhelmed by the various technical problems involved and become thoroughly disheartened in the process. When you first come across a piece of written music, though, a quick look should reveal how hard it is to play – although some pieces can be very deceptive, it has to be said.

The next thing to do is cut down the piece into smaller sections – say, eight bars in length, or even four – and play these in turn, rather than the whole piece at once. Doing this will enable you to focus on a much smaller area at once and deal with any technical mantraps you come across as part of your practice routine.

The key here is to be patient. Be prepared to invest a considerable amount of time in learning a piece, reassuring yourself that every technical obstacle you successfully overcome will help your playing overall. Don't let yourself fall into the trap of high expectations yielding poor results through impatience and frustration; instead, take everything you do at a slow, even pace. Many of my students would set themselves impossible targets – I used to call them 'personal Everests' – and I found that I could generally defuse the situation by introducing them to the concept of breaking down a piece into four-bar chunks. Just remind yourself that the answer to most problems in the practice room can be solved by the three Ps: patient, persistent practice.

Ciao, Bella

Back to navigating through a piece or a song. Remember when I mentioned learning basic music-based Italian earlier? Well, here we go.

The markings on pieces of modern music have retained some of the traditions of ancient times, and one of these traditions is that verbal directions on a piece of music should be in any other language other than English. I don't know why this is, and if anyone would like to begin a campaign for musical road signs in English then I'd willingly put my name at the top of the list, as it would save me a lot of time in the classroom. Until such a time, though,

we're pretty much stuck with things being the way they are, so you'll need to know what some of these directions actually mean in plain English.

The first one you're likely to meet is *da capo*, which means literally 'from the head' or, practically, 'from the top'. (You've probably seen jazz musicians in films say things like, 'Let's take it from the top, guys,' by which they mean, 'Let's start from the beginning.') If you see this marking in a piece of music, it means 'Play through from the beginning of the piece until you reach the end or until you're told to stop.'

There are a couple of variations on this marking, both of which are in common use, so let's explore them too, while we're here. The first of these, *da capo al fine*, means 'from the top (or head) to the end'. Now, you might think that this is perhaps a needless addition, but listen up, because it actually means something similar to regular *da capo* but not exactly what it says.

You're most likely to find *da capo al fine* towards the end of a piece. In practical terms, it actually means 'go back to the beginning and play through the piece again until you see the word *fine*, then stop'. It's just a way of directing you to repeat only a bit of the music and not the whole thing – and it saves the need to write out the same music again and waste paper. Let's save a tree, right?

Another word you need to be aware of here is *coda*, literally meaning 'tail', which turns out to be an appropriate term as it usually applies to a few bars of music that take the form of an ending or conclusion to a piece – like a stuck-on tail, in fact. The coda has its own sign, too:

This is where the other variation on *da capo* applies. *Da capo al coda* means 'go back to the beginning, play through the music until you see the coda sign and then play the coda itself'. This kind of thing, in fact:

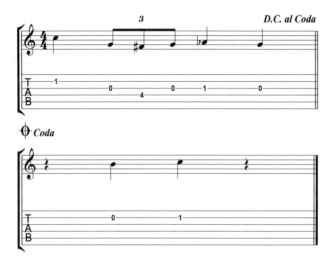

Be prepared for the fact that *da capo al whatever* is quite often abbreviated to *DC al whatever*, thus saving not only trees but ink, too.

You're probably getting the idea now that finding your way through a piece of music is a little like learning the rules to a board game like Monopoly, in which case you're certainly not far off. There are a great number of similarities between the two, in fact, although you very rarely see the direction 'Go to jail' in music scores.

My point is that, while all this Italian might seem somewhat bewildering at first, if you treat it like learning to play a board game then you'll soon pick up the rules as you go along. I certainly did. I can't remember ever sitting down and actually learning any of this; it's just stuff that I've picked up from reading through a lot of music scores. For instance, back in my youth I once played in a musical – the first time I'd ever played in a pit orchestra, in fact – and had to read my way through around 90 minutes of music. It was here that I came across another musical direction at the bottom of one page, VS (actually short for *volti subito*), which, I soon discovered, means, 'Turn over the page double-quick,' usually because your instrument does something immediately on the page turn and you really need to be ready. Sitting in an ensemble, without having had enough time to rehearse, I was really learning under fire.

So far I've talked about markings that direct you back to the beginning of a piece, but what if you need to go back to the middle and play through from there to the end? Here, you'll find yet another variation on the *da capo* theme, only this time it's *da segno*, which means 'from the sign'. The sign in question looks like this:

It's a sort of ornate capital S that looks as if it's been shoved over on its side, but if you see the direction *da segno* – or even its abbreviation *DS* – you'll have to keep your eyes peeled as you'll need to play from where this sign occurs. Then you'll need to follow the other half of the instruction, which will be either *al coda* (to the tail) or *al fine* (to the end).

There are in fact many more directions involved in the board game of written music, but these are by far the most common. If you're curious about the others, I recommend that you check out the ABRSM (Associated Board of the Royal Schools of Music)'s *AB Guide To Music Theory*, which contains a comprehensive list of them all.

As I said earlier, though, experience is really the best teacher here, but you'll no doubt find it easier to navigate through songs that actually have lyrics, as these will provide valuable reference points.

Gimme A Sign

Sorry, but we're not through with learning Italian quite yet. There are a few other things concerning the nature of music that the language of the Renaissance is used to describe.

The first of these is *dynamic markings*, which indicate how loudly or softly you're meant to be playing at various points in a piece of written music. You might be thinking that these directions aren't quite as vital as those guiding you through a piece, but there are reasons why you should at least familiarise yourself with a few of them.

Now, I realise that you'll probably already know the pieces you learn on the guitar; it's mostly in the classical world that guitarists encounter scores that they haven't heard before, so the chances are that you'll be aware of the dynamic niceties involved. However, you might be puzzled by a few of them, so here's a brief guide.

Basically, in music p refers to the Italian word *piano*, which means 'soft', and f stands for *forte*, which means 'strong' or 'loud'.

So far, so good, but obviously there are many degrees of softness and loudness, so we need signs for 'very soft' and 'very loud', too. In fact, with uncharacteristic simplicity, the music abbreviation for 'very quiet' is just p with an additional p, giving us pp. You'll probably also come across ppp and even $pppp$, indicating something that's so quiet it's almost beneath the level of human hearing.

Meanwhile, the same labelling convention applies to degrees of loudness. If you want a section to be played very loudly, you just add another f to the marking for *forte*, so ff means 'very loud', and you can even use the very unsociable $ffff$ if you really want to take the roof off. I realise that this is unlikely on an acoustic guitar, but who knows?

The last two signs we'll look at in this section apply to parts of music that need to become either gradually louder or gradually softer. Here, you might not see this indication represented by words in the score (although *crescendo* [abbreviated *cresc*] and *diminuendo* [abbreviated *dim*] are often used to indicate these respective volume changes); instead, you'll see signs like these:

Known colloquially as 'hairpins' (because, I'm led to understand, they resemble, erm, hairpins), these two signs between the staffs mean are musical shorthand for *crescendo* (on the left, meaning 'Play increasingly loudly') and *diminuendo* (on the right, meaning 'Play increasingly quietly').

Once again, I don't have room here to cover all the foreign words you're likely to find in written music – for a start, I haven't even mentioned the fact that sometimes you'll meet French and German words, too – but I've covered some of the more common ones. I would encourage you, however, to invest in a dedicated theory book, like the one published by the ABRSM I mentioned earlier, to increase your level of knowledge in this area.

Instrumental Music

To finish off this chapter, I want to talk briefly about instrumental music, which, you're probably already aware, is music without any singing or speaking. You're probably also aware of the fine tradition of instrumental music out there that has been produced by solo acoustic guitarists. To me, this is where some of the most interesting music currently available is to be found; indeed, the acoustic guitar has enjoyed something of a renaissance over the last few years as players have become more adventurous in their compositions, to the extent that we're now miles away from that hackneyed vision of a man in a shaggy jumper with an acoustic guitar on his knee, playing traditional folk music in a pub somewhere (not that there's anything wrong with this, of course!).

In terms of purely acoustic instrumental music, a few of the conventions we've examined so far are abandoned in favour of what could easily pass for those from the classical world. For a start, instead of the notion of music having distinctly different melodic and harmonic content – a melody with chordal accompaniment, for instance – in instrumental solo-guitar music the two are combined to form one part. As you approach this area of acoustic music, I advise you to abandon the notion of chord shapes – which many guitarists rely on and look upon as a sort of security blanket – and resort to the rules and conventions of harmony and composition.

This concept of music is perhaps a very advanced one, but here's a very brief insight into what actually happens inside a piece of proper acoustic instrumental music (ie not song-accompaniment playing).

Classical guitar composers didn't write their music as comprising just melody and chord symbols or labels; instead, they combined the two to form a cohesive whole. You certainly won't see chord names or boxes over the top of classical scores, as these conventions aren't relevant in the area of instrumental music. As an example, try to track down a recording of JS Bach's 'Fugue in A Minor' (BWV 1000) for classical guitar. I picked this piece in particular because it sounds like there's an awful lot going on in it. A fugue is a form of music in which a basic melody is played back against itself in the form of a canon, like the children's song 'London's Burning'. In the Bach piece, the basic melody is first played in the treble register and then in the bass while another melody is interlaced over it – which sounds like quite a challenge to play on the guitar, but you might be surprised. To begin with, there aren't any chords as such – certainly not in the way we know them – and yet harmonically everything hangs together very well. In fact, the harmony is implied rather than strummed out in the background, and yet nothing seems to be missing. The score to the piece is actually very sparse – there's a lot less going on than you might think – which is a very common characteristic of instrumental music. It's a kind of less-is-more principle – an illusion, if you like – but it's very effective.

Now, I realise that using any piece of music by JS Bach as an example is a little unfair; the man was a genius, after all, and his music is notoriously difficult to play on the guitar. The fugue in A minor is an examination piece, in fact, and you'll need some considerable technique in order to play it successfully, but it does demonstrate the same kind of harmonic approach present in much easier pieces, too. With this in mind, here's a much easier example for you to experiment with:

BAROQUE DANCE
Anon

In my experience, music from the Baroque era sounds great on both metal- and nylon-string guitar, and this piece shouldn't give you too many problems. Even if you're not keen on taking your playing in this direction, check out the recording of this piece on the accompanying CD and study the tab. You'll note that it sounds complete somehow and that any kind of traditional rhythmic accompaniment underneath the melody isn't at all necessary.

You'll also notice that the piece is credited to 'Anon', short for 'Anonymous', meaning that we don't actually know who wrote it – which is a shame, because it's a nice tune! All we know is that it was probably written over 400 years ago, in around 1600.

In any case, an awful lot of modern music for the acoustic guitar is based upon the same approach. In these pieces, gone are the traditional rules of song accompaniment; instead, the guitarist is required to play everything: melody, harmony and bass line.

That just about sums up the idea of fusing together all the individual elements of acoustic playing – chords, scales, right- and left-hand technique, etc – and I hope it's given you some idea of exactly what's going on with acoustic-guitar music at present. Before you start the workout itself, however, there's perhaps one other area to consider first.

ALTERNATE TUNINGS

Before you say anything, yes, I know that this chapter should be titled 'Alternative Tunings'; this is just one more example of traditions in music overriding any sense of logic or good sense. Just bear with me, please.

I won't bore you with the history of how exactly the standard tuning of a guitar was decided. Looked at logically, the conventional sequence of string tunings – E A D G B E – seems a little strange, as it actually prevents us from being able to play certain things, particularly in the area of chords, where it's nearly impossible to play certain chord voicings that are commonplace on the piano. There have been various attempts to implement alternative standards – for instance, 'fourths tuning', which involves raising the pitch of the B string to C and the top string to F, has often been punted as a far more logical alternative – but we guitar players are a conservative bunch and stick to standard 'Spanish' tuning, despite its shortcomings. Well, most of us do, at least...

You might have heard about guitarists using 'drop tunings' or 'tuning to a chord' as an alternative to standard tuning. This is particularly prevalent amongst the current crop of new players, who are obviously keen to explore different tunings in order to give their music an original edge. Many such players will use an alternate tuning for a couple of pieces in their repertoire while others will stick to a different tuning and rarely visit standard tuning. It's a crazy, mixed-up world. So, to round off this examination of contemporary acoustic playing, here's a brief look at a few of the more common alternate tunings around today.

Tuning To A Chord

This is probably the oldest tradition of retuning the instrument and was probably first devised in the birthplace of the blues, America's Deep South. Back in the early 1900s, when blues was just beginning to be standardised as a legitimate form of music, it was commonplace to abandon any idea of standard guitar tuning and instead to tune the instrument to a chord. This practice was originally intended to facilitate playing slide guitar, a style that's much easier to pull off when the guitar is tuned to a chord. This kind of tuning is also known as *open tuning*.

Common open-chord tunings are open G and open D, where the strings are tuned like this:

Open G: D G D G B D
Open D: D A D F♯ A D

Now, when you first look at these tunings, you'll probably notice one thing immediately: that everything you already know about chords, scales and harmony on the guitar is now entirely useless to you! This is unfortunately true, and it's certainly something that prevents an awful lot of players from exploring alternate tunings from the start; no one wants to become a beginner again and start at day one with a fresh set of chord and scale shapes. That said, I would advise you to try a couple of open tunings, at least, even if you just resort to playing barre chords all over the neck – and, if you do, remember that, on a guitar tuned to a chord, barre chords look like this:

So, if you played the open strings (in G) followed by a barre at the fifth fret, then another at the seventh, you'd have just played this...

‖ G / / / ｜ C / / / ｜ D / / / ‖

...with little or no effort at all!

Obviously, there's an awful lot more to playing open-G and -D tunings than just playing around with simple barres, and many players have become amazingly adept at working with open tunings and have produced some truly original music. Possibly the most famous of these exponents of alternate tunings is Joni Mitchell, who has never really settled on a single tuning for her guitar but instead tends to change tuning for virtually every song.

DADGAD

Drop Tuning

Another tuning alternative is to retune only one or two strings from standard tuning to enable certain chord voicings or a profound bass. Surprisingly, this approach to tuning is common even in classical guitar, where the bass string is often dropped a tone to D to give this:

D A D G B E

Not such a radical difference, maybe, but this tuning is also used in steel-string compositions, too, where it's usually known as *drop-D tuning*. Many players say that tuning this way seems to give the guitar a vastly extended bass range, even though the bass string has been dropped by only a tone.

Once again, I'd urge you to try dropping your bass string to D and experiment. Here, you don't need to alter your way of thinking about chords too much, as nothing much has changed, but try playing something in the key of D and you'll see what I mean about the range of the bass seeming to have increased by far more than just a single tone!

DADGBE

DADGAD

This is possibly the most interesting alternate tuning. As you might expect, the strings of a guitar tuned to DADGAD are tuned like this:

D A D G A D

Here, you have another chord forming your open strings, but this time, instead of a straight major chord, you've got a Dsus4 instead:

No one's exactly sure where DADGAD tuning originated, and it does seems strange to tune to a suspended chord, but it definitely has its charms. It's also described (wrongly, in my opinion) as a modal tuning or a Celtic tuning and is the foundation of a lot of great acoustic-guitar music.

Once again, all familiar reference points and landmarks are removed as both chord and scale shapes are entirely different from those associated with standard tuning. Even so, I advise you to spend a while with your guitar tuned to DADGAD; you'll probably find that you either love it or loathe it. Personally, I love it and have written a couple of pieces using it, although I don't know it as thoroughly as I do standard tuning. So, when I visit DADGAD, I do so with the full realisation that I'm a stranger in a strange land – and that all adds to its mystery somehow. I have to experiment, find my way, work things out in a way that I haven't done since I began learning, aeons ago.

Many players from diverse parts of the music style spectrum have used DADGAD tuning, and some have even made it their home, as did the late, great acoustic player Eric Roche. The tuning isn't limited to acoustic playing, either; Led Zeppelin's monster-rock epic 'Kashmir' has a riff based in DADGAD, and no one would accuse Jimmy Page of being a folk guitarist!

There are many recognised alternate tunings to explore and I definitely advise you to explore them once you've developed some basic technical skills (and once you've bought a decent tuner; all this retuning can fry the brain quicker than anything).

Before I leave the subject of altered tunings, however, I need to say a few words about a quick and easy retuning device that's available to all of us: a wonderful little mechanical device called a *capo*.

Capos

A capo is basically a little bar that clamps across the fingerboard, holding down all of the strings to form a sort of automatic barre – but one that leaves all the fingers of the left hand free, like this:

A capo in position on the guitar neck

Capos can be used at any fret and effectively give you a new set of open strings to play with. Use it at the third fret, for instance, and your open strings become this...

G   C   F   B♭   D   G

...which means that the open-position E-shape chord now becomes G major:

G

The first and most obvious use of a capo is to change the key of a guitar-accompanied song to suit a singer's voice. Singers are notorious for having vocal ranges that centre around awkward keys, and being quick-witted with a capo means not having to relearn entire chord arrangements. All you need to do is learn to regard the capo as being the nut of the guitar. They sometimes present a psychological barrier that prevents some players from getting on with them, and some rock players regard them as being far too uncool to use, but that never bothered blues legends such as Muddy Waters or Albert Collins, so I wouldn't let it bother you!

Many acoustic players use capos, and some music books will warn you when they do but some won't. I was put off from playing any of Paul Simon's music for ages because a lot of it appeared to be in E♭ – an awkward key to play in for an early learner – but then I saw some footage of him playing with a capo on the third fret of his guitar and I enjoyed one of those 'Aha!' moments.

There are basically two types of capo tablature notation: one that carries on as if the capo isn't there while telling you that there's a capo in use and where, like this...

Capo 3rd fret

...while the other 'zeroes' the capo, after which everything is notated as if it was played down at the nut, like this:

Capo 3rd fret

There is some fierce debate as to which of these methods is the most user-friendly, and I can see the benefits of both, although I must admit that the idea of zeroing the capo makes a little more sense, as it makes the music more instantly transposable; in other words, you could play it in an open position if you didn't have (or couldn't find) a capo, or you could move the capo higher or lower on the fretboard to play the piece in a different key.

Whichever way you use one, however, a capo is a great little gizmo that no acoustic player should be without. They're great for giving you a fresh set of sounds to play with if you're trying to come up with some ideas for songs or instrumentals yourself – and, as I mentioned earlier, they render you instantly singer-proof at the same time!

PART 2

THE ACOUSTIC GUITAR GYM

INTRODUCTION

Welcome to Part 2 of the *10 Minute Acoustic Guitar Workout*. This section of the book is really the heart of the matter, as it comprises the exercises that should form the first ten minutes of your daily practice routine from now on.

Each of the exercises in this section has a dual role, providing a testing area for the hands and addressing such matters as co-ordination, stamina and general dexterity. Also, each is centred around a musical concept, so while you're honing the technical side of your playing, you'll also be absorbing a lot of valuable music at the same time, and almost subliminally.

The whole concept of the ten-minute workout began as a pact between myself and my private pupils. In an hour-long lesson, the first ten minutes would be spent playing technical exercises so that I could be assured that this side of their development was on track. Of course, I was aware that exercises are the most boring things to do and that the average guitar player would rather do almost anything else instead, so the other 50 minutes of my students' lessons were spent doing something that *they* wanted to do: learn a song, prepare a solo for something they were learning with their band – anything. This enabled me to address both sides of their guitar-learning experience: I was in charge of their technical development but I was also prepared to let them choose whatever stylistic path they wanted to follow.

As a musician myself, I believe that music is music and that students can learn as much from playing through an Abba or Beatles song as they can from studying Delta blues. Even though things might appear very different on the surface, the cogs and wheels of music theory are still turning in very much the same way underneath.

Like I said, ideally your ten-minute routine should form the first part of your daily practice time, and like my students, after this you should feel free to choose what music you want to study. The workout will keep your technical side sharp and should soon produce noticeable results in your playing.

Before you start, though, I advise you to read through the section on 'Using The Charts', which contains valuable advice on making the most from the workout.

Good luck!

An Apple A Day

Embarking on any rigorous practice routine can put an awful lot of strain on the muscles and tendons in the arms and hands, so it's worth spending a few moments reading up on how to avoid injuring yourself before you begin working through the charts in this part of the book.

You've probably heard horror stories about conditions like RSI (repetitive strain injury), carpal tunnel syndrome and tendonitis that tend to dog the guitar world. Well, by following a few simple guidelines, you can generally avoid the risk of hurting yourself and keep your practising and performing fun and pain-free.

To begin with, let's bust one particular myth: there's no such thing as good pain. I don't want you to work through the pain barrier with these exercises; despite what I might have said earlier, you're not joining the guitar-playing Marines after all, and I'm certainly not going to adopt the guise of a snarling sergeant-major pushing you forward at any cost.

If at any time you experience any discomfort or unusual sensation in your hands or fingers, stop playing for a few minutes and rest your hands. This will usually do the trick, but if the condition persists then it's time to see a doctor to make sure everything's functioning normally. There's a huge difference between the warm glow we get from exercise and the actual pain that stems from the body's self-defence system telling us to stop, and you should be able to recognise the difference. It might sound like I'm overdoing the seriousness of this situation, but none of the exercises in this section should cause you any pain.

So, what sort of thing should you watch out for? For a start, be very attentive to the positions of your hands and arms at all times. Keep your wrists as straight as possible and your forearms relaxed so that your hands and arms are free from tension, which can cause them to seize up. To this end, make sure your playing position is as relaxed as possible without actually dropping the guitar.

Try to keep both your wrists as straight as possible at all times

Make sure your elbows don't poke out, too. I've seen so many players do this as they play, and it always gives them problems one way or another as it's a great source of tension. You can feel this for yourself by sitting on a chair without a guitar and sticking both elbows out in a sort of chicken-wing position. Can you feel the strain at the tops of both arms? This will actually impair your freedom of movement, so avoid it as much as you can.

In fact, there's a lot to be said for checking your playing position every so often in a mirror* just to make sure you're not lapsing into bad habits. You'd be surprised by how much you can learn about your guitar-playing posture this way. I've been horrified when confronted by some video footage of me playing – although usually it's a fashion thing rather than a matter of posture – and I've taken immediate remedial action in both respects.

Something else that a great many guitarists suffer from is back problems. These can be attributed to practising while slouched in an armchair or, worst of all, the couch-potato-type noodling position on a sofa. You're free to have fun with your guitar in any position that takes your fancy, but please, when you're doing serious practice, you need to do so on a chair with your back as straight as possible. You'll thank me in the end!

Also, if you intend to wear a strap during performance – and remember, by 'performance' I'm referring to practically any playing situation – then make sure you adjust it so that your guitar is the same height when you're sitting and standing. I've dealt with so many players who have perfected something when they're sitting down to practise only to find that they virtually have to return to the drawing board when they try to play it standing up. It might sound like a small difference, but I invite you to try playing your guitar at different heights and see for yourself what happens. You'll be surprised.

---

* If any family member catches you doing this and uses it as an excuse to hurl abuse at you, tell them I told you it was OK.

So the key things to do here are to adopt a sensible posture: keep your wrists as straight as possible and avoid hunching your back while you're playing. If you follow this advice, everything should be fine.

Using The Charts

In this next section of the book, you'll find six charts, each comprising five exercises. All of the exercises in this part are designed to be performed in two minutes, so playing five will comprise your ten-minute routine. Meanwhile, accompanying each set of exercises is a progress chart indicating how many times you need to repeat each task within the given two-minute slot, like this:

	Ex 1	Ex 2	Ex 3	Ex 4	Ex 5
A+	40	50	30	36	24
A	36	48	28	30	22
A–`	30	45	27	27	19
B+	25	42	26	23	17
B	22	38	24	19	15
B–	20	32	22	16	13
C+	15	28	18	14	10
C	10	22	14	12	7
C–	8	18	10	9	5
D+	5	12	7	6	3
D	4	6	5	4	2
D–	2	2	2	1	1

The idea is that you start at the lowest level on the chart (D–) and work your way over a period of time towards the top level (A+). As you progress through the levels, the number of times you repeat each exercise gradually increases, making things a little more challenging.

Moving from the lowest level to the highest on each chart will take you weeks, but there's no time limit in this regard and certainly no rush; I don't want you trying to set records here. The idea is that you progress at your own level, but I do want you to be strict with yourself and keep a constant check on matters like accuracy and articulation.

Now here are a few guidelines that will help you to make your progress through the charts as trouble-free as possible.

Go Somewhere Quiet

I know it's difficult to find a quiet place in the maelstrom of modern domestic living, but it's important that you practise your routine with as few distractions as humanly possible. Try to find somewhere that's free from interruption and outside noise. The correct environment ought to be just you and a guitar with no background noise from the TV or radio.

Everyone Starts At Level 1

No matter how far you've come as a player, you should really begin at the lowest level, even if you find the exercises there very easy to begin with. With these exercises, I'm trying to encourage the habit of practice as much as anything, so if feels like you're on the nursery slopes for a while, all well and good. Don't worry; things will begin to warm up before too long.

Make Practice A Routine

Try to do your workout at the same time every day. I know this might be difficult to do but it's a valuable discipline to adopt. Years ago, I was fanatically rigid with my own practice routine, to the extent that I felt really guilty if circumstances prevented me from doing it. I think I benefited from adopting this attitude, though, and since then I've advised all my students to attempt to do the same.

Keep An Eye On The Clock

Try to spend exactly the right amount of time on each exercise. Don't go on longer than necessary because you're enjoying playing something; the main point of this workout is that time is limited. Also, if you find one particular exercise easy, don't be tempted to leave it alone; in order to feel the full effects of the workout, you'll need to complete the exercises in their written sequence.

Be Your Own Adjudicator

Never be tempted to move on too fast or, worse, prematurely. The only time that you can move further ahead is when you're fluent at each of the five exercises at any one level. If one particular routine is holding you back, read the chapter 'Establishing An Effective Practice Routine' in Part 1 to find out how to diagnose problems with your playing. You might need to deal with an underlying cause like poor hand position or inaccurate fingering. Remember that finding problems with your playing in this way is a positive thing because, once you've dealt with them, you can progress.

Read The Instructions

I've tried to give clear instructions for each exercise, having learned my lesson from the notorious 'chart 1, exercise 5' in the original *10 Minute Guitar Workout* where I was obviously having a bad day and didn't get the point across. The result was an email inbox heaving from the strain!

Temporary Stoppages

Obviously there are going to be times when you're unable to keep up your practice routine due to extramusical factors like family holidays and illness. In these instances, take a few steps back before proceeding; instead of carrying on where you left off when you come back or get better, drop down a level for a day or two to bring yourself back up to speed before pushing ahead.

Finish What You Started

Like every good doctor says, the medicine works only if you finish the course, so try your best to make a commitment to finishing all six charts. None of the exercises calls for Olympic feats of strength and endurance; rest assured that I haven't made any of the charts impossible to finish in the hope of breeding my own acoustic-guitar-playing master race!

Don't Expect Instant Results

The charts here are graded to ensure progress, but the chances are that it will be a while before you notice anything different in your day-to-day playing life. Don't become despondent about this; the chances are that friends and family will notice a change in your playing before you do.

Keep A Check On What You're Doing

There's a recording of each of the exercises on the accompanying CD, and it's a good idea to keep checking to make sure you're going in the right direction, musically, with these exercises. It's very easy to go off along the wrong path and not realise it until you're hopelessly lost, so review your progress every so often to make sure you're still on track.

Progress At Your Own Pace

I know I've said this before but there's no limit to the amount of time you can spend on any one chart (apart from your daily ten-minute deadline, of course). Judging by all the mail I've received since the publication of the *10 Minute Guitar Workout*, it's not uncommon to spend months working through each level, but don't worry if this is the case with you, as any rate of progress is fine. I'd rather you be too slow about things rather than rush forward.

Pick Or Fingers?

Despite the fact that most of these exercises here are designed for fingerstyle technique, I've given alternative instructions where necessary so that it's possible to do the workout with a plectrum if need be.

More Questions?

I think I've covered everything you need to know before you begin your workout, but if you have any questions at this point, or if any crop up as you work through the charts, email me at info@davidmead.net and I'll try to help you out.

CHART 1

CD Track 10

Welcome to the beginning of your daily ten-minute workout. There are five exercises here, each designed to address a different area of technique, and with a little ear training thrown in for good measure!

The chart on the right indicates how many times you should perform each exercise within the time allowed. Begin at the time required to be at a level of D– and work your way up to A+, checking constantly to make sure that what you're playing is accurate. Take your time and don't be tempted to rush forwards too soon. Expect to spend a few days at each level before moving upwards.

If you're in any doubt as to how any of the exercises should sound, the CD has a recording of me playing each of them at different speeds to give you a good idea of what to aim for.

You'll find some exercises more difficult than others, but spend the same amount of time on each, no matter what. Don't move up the chart until all of the exercises at are running smoothly at the same level. Also, please read the section titled 'An Apple A Day' in the 'Introduction' to Part 2 before beginning this programme, as it contains essential advice on avoiding repetitive strain injury and associated ailments.

	Ex 1	Ex 2	Ex 3	Ex 4	Ex 5
A+	40	50	30	36	24
A	36	48	28	30	22
A–	30	45	27	27	19
B+	25	42	26	23	17
B	22	38	24	19	15
B–	20	32	22	16	13
C+	15	28	18	14	10
C	10	22	14	12	7
C–	8	18	10	9	5
D+	5	12	7	6	3
D	4	6	5	4	2
D–	2	2	2	1	1

Maximum two minutes per exercise

Exercise 1
Warm-up

This exercise is designed to function as a wake-up call for both hands and fingers and entails moving between the chords C major and G7 using a very specific right-hand fingering. The chances are that it will take you a few days to become accustomed to the chord change itself, so don't get disheartened if things seem very awkward to begin with. You should correct any buzzy notes by carefully checking your left-hand and finger positions.

PICK USERS

When playing this exercise with a pick, strum the two chords with the right hand but keep a very careful eye on what your left hand is getting up to as you do so.

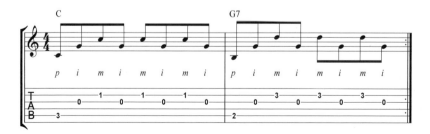

Chart 1

Exercise 2
Arpeggio

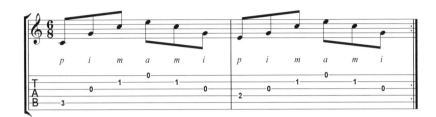

The second exercise in your routine is an *arpeggio*, which means it's just a chord you should play one note at a time. This is a great exercise for making sure that your right-hand fingers are coming on line. Make sure you stick to the fingering shown here, and when you first start it keep checking back to make sure nothing has slipped and that all your fingers are still on their assigned strings. Don't be surprised if your ring finger, *a*, is a slow learner to begin with; most players experience some resistance here at first.

PICK USERS

Using a plectrum makes this a string-crossing exercise – essential for learning how to play interesting song accompaniments.

Exercise 3
Scale

This exercise gives you a chance to look at using your right-hand fingers for playing melody. First of all we'll begin with the strong *i* and *m* partnership on an A major scale in the open position. (This means we're including some open strings in the scale.) Pay specific attention to the right-hand fingers: these must play in a strictly alternating fashion at all times. Remember that you're acquiring some very important technical skills here, so don't be put off if the exercise feels strange at the start. You'll soon pick things up.

PICK USERS

Treat this exercise as a test for co-ordination. Use up- and downstrokes with the plectrum alternately and keep checking to make sure your playing is strictly alternate before even thinking about moving up the chart.

Exercise 4
Chromatic Exercise

This is a deliberate finger-twister for both hands. It's basically a chromatic pattern over two strings involving, once again, some specific fingering. Chromatic exercises are notoriously hard on the ears, but remember that the chromatic scale is the musical alphabet and becoming familiar with it is essential for developing a deeper understanding of how melody works.

PICK USERS

Once again, treat this exercise as a chance to check on the co-ordination between your hands. Aim for absolute precision at all times and speeds.

Exercise 5
Harmonised Scale

This is essentially another scale exercise, but this time to be played as chords! Later charts exploit whole scales, but just to get you acclimatised to the basic idea this one requires you to play a fragment of the C harmonised scale. Here you'll be changing chords on every beat, which will definitely take you a while to get used to, and because of this difficulty the initial levels on the chart don't contain too many repeats.

This is an excellent way to build stamina and increase fluency, so take your time and keep checking back with the CD to make sure you're dead on track.

PICK USERS

Simply strum each chord. This exercise is more of a challenge to the left hand than to the right.

Once you can play all of the exercises in this chart comfortably at the A+ level, move on to Chart 2.

CHART 2

CD Track 11

After working through Chart 1, you should find that your fingers are now much more 'sure-footed' and your stamina increased, too. I'm hoping that by now your ten-minute daily routine has developed into a habit and that you're hungry for more challenges!

In any case, each of the exercises in this chart is a development of those you've just been doing; they just involve more diabolical fingerings and tend to cover more of the fretboard than the exercises in Chart 1.

My advice here is the same as before: proceed slowly and keep checking against the CD to make sure you're on the right track. The chart has taken into consideration the fact that it will take you a few days to become familiar with the new exercises, so things might appear to slow down initially. This is actually no bad thing, as it will give you time to make sure everything is up and running correctly before you increase speed.

	Ex 1	Ex 2	Ex 3	Ex 4	Ex 5
A+	40	24	12	29	12
A	37	22	11	25	11
A–	33	19	10	22	10
B+	27	16	9	19	9
B	23	14	7	15	8
B–	19	12	6	13	7
C+	15	10	5	10	6
C	12	8	5	8	4
C–	9	7	3	6	4
D+	7	5	2	5	2
D	5	4	2	3	2
D–	3	2	1	2	1

Maximum two minutes per exercise

Exercise 1
Warm-up

This exercise is a variation on Chart 1, Exercise 1, so your left hand should already be familiar with it. The big change here is the introduction of the right-hand ring finger, which can be very uncooperative to begin with, so don't be surprised if it doesn't do anything you ask it to for a while. It will improve as long as you're patient. Just keep things really slow initially and you should find that it soon starts to respond.

PICK USERS

Use this exercise as a supplementary arpeggio/cross-picking workout.

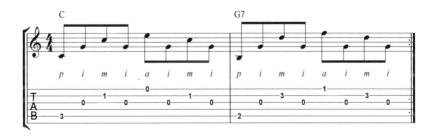

Exercise 2
Arpeggio

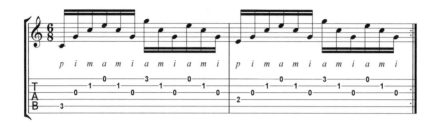

This is a real finger-twister for the right hand. It's deliberately designed so that order emerges out of chaos; the fingerpicking pattern might look a little out of the ordinary, but it will really give your fingers some independence – essential for good song accompaniment. Keep a very careful watch on the ring finger, *a*: don't let your middle finger help it out when you play the fretted note on the top string.

PICK USERS

This exercise is also a kind of finger-twister for the plectrum. It's a string-crossing nightmare that will really begin to develop your pick control.

Exercise 3
Scale

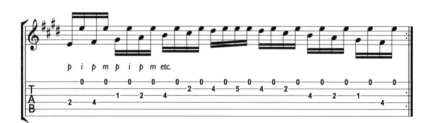

This exercise calls for you to play an open-position E major scale with the thumb while fingers *i* and *m* play the top E string. It's very important here to make sure that fingers *i* and *m* are playing strictly alternately at all times, as this will help you to develop a lot of fluency when playing melody lines in the future. If you're in any doubt as to how it should sound, listen to the accompanying CD.

PICK USERS

Play the scale as written, using the pick to play both the low strings and the top E. This involves a lot of moving around with the pick, which will test your accuracy, but it will also help you to build a very solid picking technique.

Chart 2

Exercise 4
Chromatic Exercise

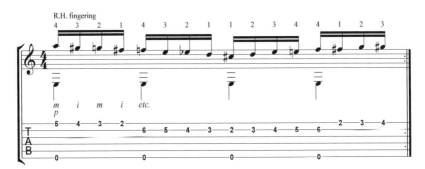

This exercises makes use of what's known in music-speak as a *pedal tone* – ie, a repeating note in either the upper or lower register – and it's designed to improve co-ordination and promote strength in the fingers of both hands. As always, keep a very careful check on your right-hand fingers and make sure they're all working on their nominated strings.

PICK USERS

You can use this exercise as another diabolical cross-picking exercise!

Exercise 5
Harmonised Scale

This is another harmonised scale – A major, in fact – but this time you'll be playing it all along the fretboard, with seven chord positions (well, eight if you include the repeated A at the top of the fingerboard) to master in a quick-fire set of changes.

The subliminal effect of this exercise is that it enables you to hear a scale played as chords, and if you refer back to 'The Right Approach To Learning Chords', you'll see how important this is for your burgeoning musical awareness.

PICK USERS

Pick each of the chords one string at a time. No strumming allowed!

When you reach level A+ in all exercises, proceed to Chart 3.

CHART 3

CD Track 12

I'm going to slow things right down again for a few days and give you a chance to feel your way into this new area. The exercises in this section are all linear developments of those you found in Charts 1 and 2, so you'll no doubt find them all both familiar and strange at once.

It's a good idea to listen hard to the CD while you read the instructions for each of the exercises here to make sure you know exactly what's expected of you.

Exercise 1
Warm-up

Here's another fingering pattern for the C–G7 warm-up routine. It takes the form of a sort of forwards-and-backwards rolling motion and is another test of your ring finger's endurance. The watchword here is *evenness* – there shouldn't be any jagged edges, just smooth, flowing notes. It's probably helpful to practise this one with a metronome to ensure that the timing is on course.

PICK USERS

Play this exercise just as it's written, using alternate strokes with the pick.

	Ex 1	Ex 2	Ex 3	Ex 4	Ex 5
A+	18	36	18	24	12
A	17	34	17	23	11
A–	16	32	16	21	10
B+	14	29	14	19	9
B	13	27	13	16	8
B–	11	24	12	14	7
C+	9	20	11	12	6
C	7	17	9	9	5
C–	5	13	6	6	4
D+	4	7	5	5	3
D	2	4	3	3	2
D–	1	2	1	2	1

Maximum two minutes per exercise

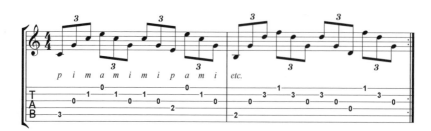

Chart 3

Exercise 2
Arpeggio

This E minor arpeggio requires you to leave the safe confines of the first few frets and move up to the fourth position (ie with your first finger on the fourth fret). It involves an additional layer of acrobatic skill in that the fingers on your left hand will have to stretch between the G and the B on the top string. Take this slowly at first – and try not to move your hand, letting the fingers do the work instead. If this isn't possible to begin with, make sure that any movement in the left hand is minimal.

PICK USERS

Play this exercise with alternate strokes at all times.

Exercise 3
Scale

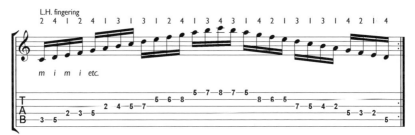

This is what's known as a *closed-position scale* (ie one with no open strings), and here the range has been increased so that the scale spans two octaves instead of just one. Because this requires the left hand to move around a lot more than previously, I've tried to keep things as simple as possible for the right, so it's fingers *i* and *m* all the way, as before. Keep checking the left-hand fingering, though, as any mistakes in this department will be difficult to correct later on.

PICK USERS

Play the exercise with alternate picking.

Exercise 4
Chromatic Exercise

This chromatic exercise offers what's perhaps an unusual alternative for the fingering in your right hand. Alternating between finger *i* and the thumb, *p*, might not be exactly conventional, but it's used a fair amount of the time. Remember what I told you when we were looking at the right hand in Part 1? Many guitarists play with whatever finger is handy, and this particular exercise will introduce you to that tradition splendidly!

PICK USERS

Another alternate-picking chromatic exercise to come to terms with!

Exercise 5
Harmonised Scale

Here's another harmonised-scale exercise, but this one includes a twist. Instead of full chords, it requires you to play sixths up the fretboard but keep an open G ringing at all times. It probably sounds harder than it is, and I'd recommend that you listen to the example on the CD before going any further.

The subliminal ear-training value here is that you get to hear how all of the 'chords' you're playing relate back to their key note or root.

PICK USERS

Try to incorporate the open G between cross-picking the sixths up the fretboard.

As with the other charts, don't proceed to Chart 4 before you can perform every exercise here comfortably at A+ level.

CHART 4

CD Track 13

You're now halfway through the ten-minute workout and should be feeling that you're making real progress. With any luck, you're finding that the fingers on both of your hands are co-operating and generally following orders as they should. From here on, things begin to get a little more difficult, although I've built in some orientation time to the new exercises to give you a few days to get things rolling.

	Ex 1	Ex 2	Ex 3*	Ex 4	Ex 5
A+	10	24	30	9	8
A	9	22	29	8	7
A−	8	20	27	7	7
B+	7	17	25	6	6
B	6	15	22	5	6
B−	5	12	20	5	5
C+	4	10	17	4	4
C	3	7	14	3	3
C−	2	5	10	2	2
D+	2	4	7	2	2
D	1	2	3	1	1
D−	1	1	1	1	1

* Ex 3a follows the timings for Ex 3.

Maximum two minutes per exercise

Exercise 1
Warm-up

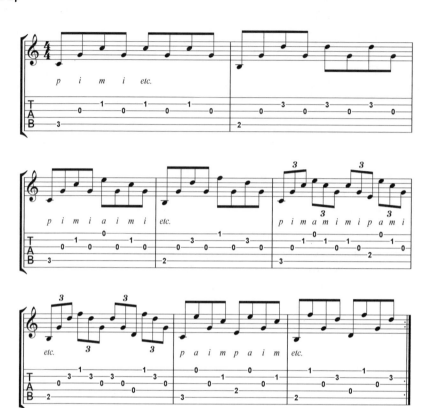

So what's going on here, exactly? Well, I thought it might be fun to review all of the warm-up exercises we've looked at so far, so I've stitched everything together into one routine. Your fingers will recognise all of the exercises from the previous charts and the new variation shouldn't give you any trouble, but you'll probably find that the rapid changing of the right-hand fingerings will cause some initial hiccups, so take things slowly!

PICK USERS

Follow the music and play all examples as arpeggios. You might have to leave out a couple of bass notes here in order to keep the flow going.

Chart 4

Exercise 2
Arpeggio

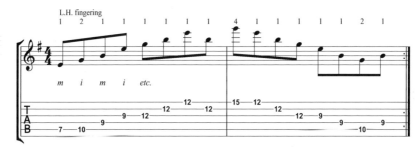

Don't worry; I haven't connected all of the previous arpeggios into one single diabolical daisy chain like I did in Exercise 1! True, this one's a little further up the fretboard – a few more steps away from familiarity – but it's still in E minor and contains only *two* position changes to negotiate. This kind of thing happens regularly in instrumental music, so being able to play this kind of passage is another essential skill to add to your rapidly growing collection.

PICK USERS

This exercise should be played with alternate picking at all times.

Exercise 3
Scale

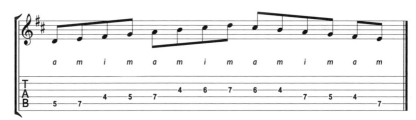

You might be looking at this scale exercise and thinking to yourself, '*One* octave? Are you sure?' Don't worry; I'm not taking this back to earlier levels. Take a look at the right-hand fingering. Now is the time to introduce your ring finger, *a*, into melody playing, and I guarantee that this exercise is much harder than it looks. You're alternating between all three right-hand fingers like this – *a m i m a* – and it will definitely take you a while to get this exercise up and running. The left hand can enjoy a bit of a rest here!

PICK USERS

Omit this exercise and instead play the alternative below.

Exercise 3a

Exercise 4
Chromatic Exercise

This one's a full six-string chromatic-scale exercise. I can't overstate the importance of the chromatic scale in music: not only does it teach you where all the notes are in any one hand position but it's also an essential reference point for the ears. Watch the left-hand fingering carefully here; I went easy on the left hand in the previous exercise, but here it really has to watch where it's going at all times.

This time, it's the right hand that has a slightly easier route to follow, as we're using only fingers *i* and *m*.

PICK USERS

Use alternate picking!

Chart 4

Exercise 5
Harmonised Scale

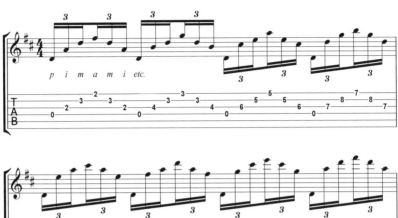

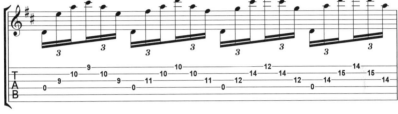

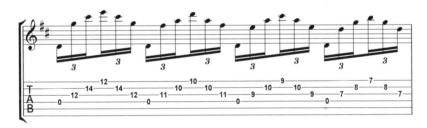

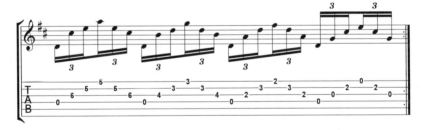

This harmonised scale sequence is in the key of D major and uses only the top three strings. It contains more vital information for the ears, and it's a good workout for the left hand, with all those position changes. Many melodies are harmonised using this system and so this kind of training will stand you in very good stead for the future.

PICK USERS

Alternate between playing this exercise as chords and arpeggios for a real workout!

CHART 5

CD Track 14

Welcome to the penultimate chart of this workout. You should definitely have noticed improvements in your overall technique by now, although the effects might still be subtle. You should be finding, however, that it takes less time to learn a song, because you're finding it easier to play and a lot of the technical difficulties seem easier to overcome.

In any case, Chart 5 is another lateral extension of what we've been doing so far – more scale- and arpeggio-based exercises with some devious right-hand fingerings thrown in to keep you on your toes!

Exercise 1
Warm-up

In direct contrast to the mammoth warm-up from the beginning of the previous chart, here's a single finger-twister to get those right-hand digits working. As usual, pay special attention to the fingering instructions and begin at the lowest level, even if it feels very easy. It's essential to give yourself a run-up to exercises like this to ensure that they deliver the maximum benefit.

PICK USERS

Play this exercise with alternate picking throughout. You'll gain a lot of pick control from working with exercises like this one!

	Ex 1	Ex 2	Ex 3	Ex 4	Ex 5
A+	24	25	12	10	8
A	23	23	11	9	7
A–	21	22	11	8	7
B+	20	19	10	7	6
B	18	15	9	6	6
B–	14	12	8	5	5
C+	11	10	6	4	5
C	9	7	5	3	4
C–	7	5	4	2	3
D+	6	4	2	2	2
D	4	2	1	1	2
D–	2	1	1	1	1

Maximum two minutes per exercise

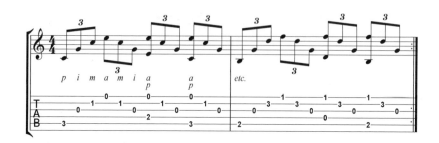

Chart 5

Exercise 2
Arpeggio

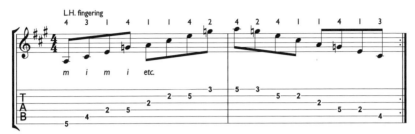

For this exercise, you'll be looking at your first dominant-seventh arpeggio in this workout. It's a two octave arpeggio, in fact, so you'll be covering a lot of ground with this one, and it's very good for developing left- and right-hand co-ordination and general visualisation on the fingerboard. Arpeggios are very important for ear development, too, as they contain the most important notes from the scale, so after spending a few weeks with this one you should be able to spot a dominant-seventh arpeggio by ear with ease!

PICK USERS

Alternate picking throughout.

Exercise 3
Scale

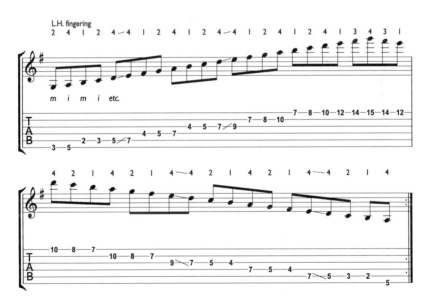

Here's the first three-octave scale – a G major scale – in this workout. As this exercise poses quite a challenge for the left hand, I'll restrict the fingering in the right hand to fingers *i* and *m* to give you a chance to pay more attention to what's happening on the fretboard. Remember to relax at all times, as tension in either hand, forearm or shoulder will prevent you from achieving a good level of fluency.

PICK USERS

Concentrate on making sure that your alternate picking is accurate. It's easy to focus so much on the left-hand fingering here that picking inaccuracies slip past.

Exercise 4
Chromatic Exercise

Well, I was easy on your right hand during the last exercise, so I'm going to make up for it here. As far as the left hand is concerned, it's another day at the office – a chromatic scale very much like the one you had in the previous chart – except that this one begins on a different note. Not to forget, of course, that at first you'll be playing it a lot more slowly than before. It's the right hand that will be doing most of the work, though, as this exercise requires you to play the scale using fingers *a*, *m* and *i* in sequence. This will definitely pose some initial co-ordination problems, but take your time and have patience. After spending a few weeks on this exercise, most of the right-hand fingerings you come across in music will seem really easy!

PICK USERS

Double-pick each note of this exercise (ie two pick strokes per scale note), beginning with an upstroke as opposed to the more regular downstroke.

Chart 5

Exercise 5
Harmonised Scale

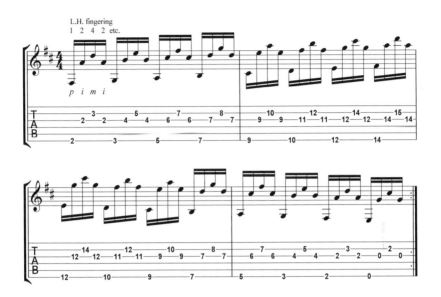

Here's another harmonised scale, this one in the key of D major again, but this time in what's known as *first inversion*. In other words, instead of having the root note of the chord in the bass, you'll be playing the third. This produces a much softer-sounding series of chords that are great for harmonising melodies.

PICK USERS

Alternate picking at all times.

If you've managed to reach A + level in each of these exercises, it's time to move on to the final chart in the workout.

CHART 6

CD Track 15

This is the final chart in the workout, and as you'd expect the exercises now reach their peak in terms of complexity and difficulty. There's nothing here that's impossible or that requires superhuman levels of ability to perform, but when you reach the A+ level in this chart you'll qualify as a real acoustic-guitar athlete!

As you begin the exercises here, take time to make sure everything's working properly; put your playing under the microscope while the exercises are still 'in neutral' around the D– level. Make sure that your hand positions are still correct – keep an eye on your posture and watch out for tension, etc – and re-read the section on self-diagnosis to make sure that any problems you have are sorted out on the workbench before they become ingrained and begin to influence your playing overall.

	Ex 1	Ex 2	Ex 3	Ex 4	Ex 5
A+	6	20	12	9	5
A	5	19	11	8	4
A–	5	18	10	7	4
B+	4	16	9	6	4
B	4	14	8	5	3
B–	4	12	7	4	3
C+	3	10	6	4	3
C	3	8	5	3	2
C–	3	6	4	2	2
D+	2	4	2	2	1
D	2	2	2	1	1

Maximum two minutes per exercise

Chart 6

Exercise 1
Warm-up

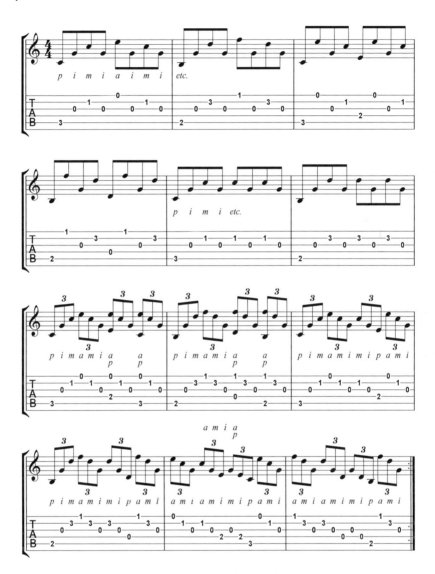

This warm-up reviews every combination of right-hand fingering we've looked at so far – and adds another one just for good measure. Such a warm-up routine is excellent for waking the fingers up, as the constant changes in right-hand fingering really keep things feeling fresh. You need to aim for 100 per cent accuracy here, something that will prove harder and harder as the speed of the exercise increases.

PICK USERS

You won't be able to achieve the same levels of speed as the fingerstyle players here. Instead, practise using a metronome and increase your speed gradually until you've reached a satisfactory level of fluency at around 120bpm.

Exercise 2
Arpeggio

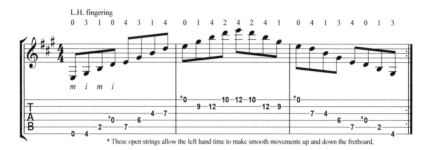

* These open strings allow the left hand time to make smooth movements up and down the fretboard.

The arpeggio exercise for this chart covers three octaves, so your left hand will be travelling quite a distance here. As usual, pay special attention to the fingering and keep checking back during the initial levels to make sure nothing's slipped and that everything remains on course.

PICK USERS

Use alternate picking throughout. This is really a workout for the left hand.

Exercise 3
Scale

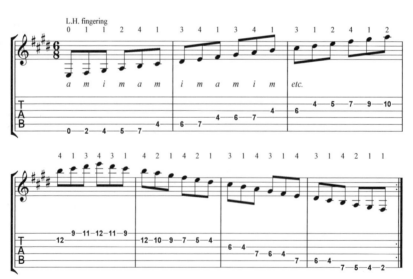

This exercise takes the form of a three-octave E major scale that uses *a–m–i* fingering throughout. By now, you should have managed to iron out most of the awkwardness with this particular fingering, but make sure it's actually 'circular' and that you're not using the same finger for two consecutive notes, which is an easy trap to fall into and one that's very difficult to correct if not caught early enough.

Try to make sure that all the position changes with the left hand are smooth, too. You shouldn't be able to hear them at all at any speed.

PICK USERS

Alternate picking throughout.

Chart 6

Exercise 4
Chromatic Exercise

This one probably represents the mother of all chromatic exercises. It begins on the bass E string and requires you to work your way up to the E at the 12th fret on the top string. You might think that the left-hand fingering here is very eccentric – after all, playing a scale on a single string seems a little too athletic when there are alternate fingerings available – but it's all good practice, and it's a real test of fluency, too. You shouldn't be able to hear any breaks in the flow as those notes proceed up the neck; instead, it should sound like one continuous stream. Have a listen to Track 15 on the CD if you need an aural nudge.

PICK USERS

This exercise is a real challenge for the pick, too!

Exercise 5
Harmonised Scale

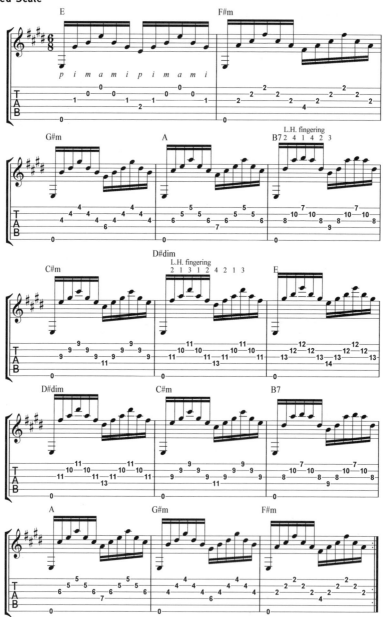

As you might expect, the last exercise in the workout is no slouch, either! It's another harmonised scale, this time in E major and with some fancy right-hand fingering thrown in.

It's no coincidence that we've looked at the keys of C, A, G, E and D in each harmonised-scale exercise; refer back to 'The Right Approach To Learning Chords' to remind yourself how important these particular chord shapes are.

PICK USERS

Try to follow the ornate fingering with your pick, but bear in mind that you won't be able to reach the top levels this way. Where playing arpeggio-based material is concerned, any race between fingers and pick is bound to end in a victory for the fingers!

Chart 6

Well, that's it. You've completed the workout. Well done! The technical facility in your right and left hands should be polished to a bright shine, and you're now ready to take on the world. What lies ahead is really up to you, but I encourage you to learn more about music theory as well as to push on with trying to play ever more challenging music.

Try to keep the musical and technical sides of your learning in balance at all times, and be sure to keep asking questions about what's happening *inside* the music you play.

Good luck!

PART 3

WHAT NEXT?

HOW GOOD IS GOOD ENOUGH?

This is something that I'm asked often. Just how good is good enough? How do you know when you can safely stop practising a piece and be sure that you're going to give a good performance of it? How well do players actually *know* the pieces in their repertoire?

Let's get one thing straight: everyone makes mistakes. I've witnessed various guitar legends miss notes, fluff chords, hit the wrong strings or experience some similar mishap during a live concert, and it reassured me that they were human, after all. But you can bet that the cause of such a dilemma wasn't down to being under-prepared or only half-knowing the piece they were playing; there's a big difference between doing the job well but making the smallest gaffe along the way and turning in a truly amateurish performance.

Everyone acknowledges that you need to practise in order to progress. In 'Establishing An Effective Practice Routine' in Part 1, I lay out all the principles involved in making sure that this precious time isn't wasted and give the advice that progressive practising is the only type that will make any real difference. So what actually goes wrong? How can you play through a song or piece of music dozens of times and still make mistakes when you try to play it in front of friends, your teacher or, horror or horrors, an audience? How come it's right when you're there by yourself but the gremlins descend if the cat wanders through the room?

Hopefully I'll have answered all of these questions by the time we're through, but first I want to tell you a little story.

In 1985 I began a course of classical guitar lessons under a very wise teacher by the name of Robert Jones. At that time I was already playing in a couple of bands and doing the occasional solo jazz gig, but I wanted to learn a little about classical guitar for two reasons: because it would improve my music reading and because I thought it would spruce up my fingerstyle technique.

Until this time, I'd taught myself the guitar by ear, and although I could read music up to a point, having had piano lessons as a child, I thought that plunging into an area of guitar playing I knew nothing about would force me to read the music from the page and not cheat and pick up everything by ear. I also played jazz guitar fingerstyle but was always in a state of complete awe when I saw or heard a classical player in concert. I knew that the technique a classical guitarist used could be adopted to play jazz, even if it did need a bit of tweaking to adapt it for metal strings.

So Robert took me through scores of classical pieces, and the method he used was always the same: we'd spend the lesson reading through a piece of music as he made suggestions concerning fingering, hand position, etc, and then I'd go away and spend the week practising it. The following week, I'd play through the piece as well as I could and then we'd instantly move on to another piece. I thought that perhaps we were going too fast, but Robert assured me that this was the way it should be done. He told me that once we'd covered the basic 'engineering' side of a piece it was up to me to work at it; his job was done. I'd only be able to keep a sharp edge on my playing, he told me, if we continually moved forward. In addition to this, he told me one of the most profound truths of playing guitar, that you in fact learn a piece at two levels: first you learn to *play* it and then you learn to *perform* it. He told me that learning to play a piece – getting the fingering right and generally making the piece work at a basic mechanical level – actually takes only a relatively short time, whereas honing it to performance quality takes a further few months.

I must admit that for many years I didn't fully understand what he meant – and it was only by proving him right on many occasions that I finally learned this most important lesson.

For instance, I was once asked to give an illustrated talk at a public school in Ipswich on the development of the guitar, so I devised a programme in which I would start on classical guitar and play a piece by the Baroque composer Robert de Visée and then move on to metal-string acoustic and finally on to electric. When I told my teacher of my intentions, he said I wasn't yet ready to perform the de Visée, despite the fact I could play it with no problems. I therefore decided to go ahead and perform it anyway, and looking back it was a real white-knuckle ride when I did. I didn't really understand the difference between playing and performing at that point, so while I was able to slog through to the end of the piece it certainly wasn't a performance I'd like anyone to remember.

On other occasions during my formative years as a player, I made similar errors of judgement and found that I was struggling with various pieces purely because I didn't really know them well enough to offer a good performance – and gradually it dawned upon me exactly what my teacher had been telling me.

You see, the difference between playing and performing is the same as that between having an acquaintance and a good friend: you need to know a piece really well before you can expect to be able to see the bigger picture and bring out all of its subtleties in a performance.

In later years, I got this point over to my students by likening it to learning to drive a car. At the beginning, you're concerned with so many different processes that all your powers of concentration are completely tied up. You still make mistakes and occasionally panic at the thought that you're driving this potentially lethal lump of metal on the public highway. You fully realise that you don't yet know enough to deal with anything out of the ordinary on the road, and it's ages before you slowly begin to assimilate everything and turn driving into one single, calculated action.

So, if I see a student trying to play a piece and I notice that they're struggling with it, I tell them that they're still looking for the gearstick or still gripping the wheel and aren't yet ready to be let loose on the road.

In order to get to that stage where playing a piece looks effortless, you really have to work hard and practise methodically, making sure that you iron out all of a piece's horror spots by dealing with them in a practical way. As I said in 'Establishing An Effective Practice Routine', you need to haul these minor flaws onto the workbench and deal with them or they'll never go away.

The trick is to realise this difference between practising and performing and never to stop practising a piece when you think you've nailed it well enough, because well enough simply won't do. I tell my students that they need to learn a piece so that playing it goes way beyond merely remembering it; they need to know it on such a fundamental level that it becomes instinctive.

If you want to know the difference between those two levels of learning, just ask yourself where the brake pedal is in your car. I guarantee that it will take you longer to remember where it is than it would take you to find it if a child ran out in front of your car. That's what I mean by knowing something by instinct. Even if you're intending only to play a piece to friends, rather than perform it publicly to a paying audience, you'll still need to do the work to move past the mechanical level where you're still worrying about fingering positions and the odd chord change and take your knowledge of the piece to the level at which you can visualise it as a whole in your head, get into it and play it from the inside. Remember the saying 'If it looks like you're working, you're not working hard enough'? Well, I'd translate that to 'If you're worrying about where the next chord is, or even what it is, you really shouldn't be playing that particular piece in public.'

Playing Live

The idea of playing in public is an absolute nightmare for some people – and this fear usually has nothing to do with their ability to play. I've known some very competent players who never want to play in public because the idea terrifies them. Fair enough; playing live isn't for everyone, and if the idea fills you with dread then perhaps you're best off avoiding it.

At one summer school where I was teaching, a pupil bolted for home on the afternoon of the student concert because he simply couldn't face it, while others insisted that they had family commitments they'd only just remembered 24 hours before their performance. I never try to talk anyone into performing if they don't want to – it's an area in which I'm far from qualified to advise anyone, after all – but any students who stayed and played in the concert that summer all experienced the same thing: a feeling that they'd overcome a huge hurdle. A performance doesn't even have to be spotless, either; just the fact that you've had a chance to put all your hard work and arduous practice to work can really benefit you on a psychological and, dare I say it, spiritual level.

The real tragedy is when someone really wants to be able to play live but finds themselves paralysed with fear at the thought of it. Here, though, help is at hand in the shape of a book by Barry Green and Timothy Gallwey entitled *The Inner Game Of Music*, which explores the reasons behind performance anxiety and includes lessons that deal with silencing those inner critical voices that urge you to fail. For many, knowing that this type of thing is an acknowledged part of performing is a major relief and represents the first step towards dealing with it. If you find yourself in this situation, I urge you to find a copy of the book and read it.

I think that the most valuable advice I was ever given about performing live went something like this: When you go out on stage in front of an audience, they want to see you succeed. They've come out for a fun evening to listen to some nice music; they're not sitting there, hoping you'll screw up. If you're at all nervous, tell the audience. You'll practically be able to feel them urging you on.

Another book that I wholeheartedly encourage you to add to your library is Philip Toshio Sudo's *Zen Guitar*, a highly unusual but ultimately very inspiring book that looks at what goes on in the background as people learn to play guitar. It's packed with great advice on how to become a player in the real sense, and it does so without reference to a single scale diagram or chord box.

Playing Through Mistakes

This is standard advice in classical music, and yet I rarely hear it outside that field. In fact, it goes hand in hand with what I've already said about really knowing a piece well enough to deal with any errors that occur, and it also ties in with my learning-to-drive analogy.

Imagine you're a learner driver trying to deal with black ice. You're already so submerged in the new experience of driving that anything unexpected will probably throw you completely and you'll lose control. Something like black ice is hard enough for even the more experienced driver to deal with, and yet most of us can, to some extent. So,

if you're playing through a piece in public while you're still figuratively looking for the gearstick, the odds are stacked against you. Knowing the piece well is the equivalent of being an experienced and able motorist, in that when something goes wrong you can correct your mistake quickly, without thinking about it. Often, the audience won't even notice – unless you draw attention to it yourself.

The worst thing you can do if you hit a curve too fast while playing is to give in to it and stop or falter. The only thing to do is carry on as if nothing has happened – literally, to play through your mistake. In music examinations, you aren't penalised too harshly when you make a mistake if the examiner thinks that you've dealt with it well enough. If you become flustered, panic and grind to a halt, they'll think that you don't know the piece well enough and will mark you down. Just remember what I said at the beginning of this chapter: everyone makes mistakes, but the real pro can pick him- or herself up and carry on without a problem.

In conclusion, let me say that I truly hope that this book has been some help to you as you navigate music's murky waters. I hope you're able to enjoy the new skills you've learned and that you go on to bring some beautiful music into the world.